THE POTPOURRI GARDENER

The Potpourri Gardener

Theodore James, Jr.

PHOTOGRAPHY BY

Harry Haralambou

COLLIER BOOKS
MACMILLAN PUBLISHING COMPANY   NEW YORK

MAXWELL MACMILLAN CANADA
TORONTO

MAXWELL MACMILLAN INTERNATIONAL
NEW YORK   OXFORD   SINGAPORE   SYDNEY

Collier Books
Macmillan Publishing Company
866 Third Avenue
New York, NY 10022

Maxwell Macmillan Canada, Inc.
1200 Eglinton Avenue East
Suite 200
Don Mills, Ontario M3C 3N1

Macmillan Publishing Company is part of the Maxwell
Communication Group of Companies.

Library of Congress Cataloging-in-Publication Data
James, Theodore.
The potpourri gardener / Theodore James, Jr.; photography by
Harry Haralambou. — 1st Collier Books ed.
p.   cm.
Includes bibliographical references (p.   ) and index.
ISBN 0-02-052293-2
1. Fragrant gardens.   2. Potpourris (Scented floral mixtures)
3. Aromatic plants.   I. Title.
[SB454.3.F7J35   1992]   92-29764   CIP
635.9'68—dc20

Macmillan books are available at special discounts for bulk purchases
for sales promotions, premiums, fund-raising, or educational use.
For details, contact:

Special Sales Director
Macmillan Publishing Company
866 Third Avenue
New York, NY 10022

First Collier Books Edition 1993

Design by Janet Tingey

10   9   8   7   6   5   4   3   2   1

Printed in the United States of America

To Marietta Silvestre and Sue Blair

Contents

Acknowledgments

We are very grateful for the assistance and interest we have received from friends, family, and neighbors, as well as various commercial enterprises that have assisted us in producing this book. We wish to acknowledge their kind cooperation.

Mr. and Mrs. Guy Heater; Francis B. Mooney; the Herb Lady, Barbara Harrington, Southold, N.Y.; Mr. and Mrs. Stanton Simm; J's Floral Fantasy, Peconic, N.Y.; Krupski's Pumpkin Farm, Cutchogue, N.Y.; Olde Towne Florist, Southold, N.Y.; David Palladini and Sherry Schreiber; Alfred and Delfina Smith; Pierre Bennerup; Leila Combs Leathers; L. Herndon Werth; Duncan and Barbara Hoxworth; Ray Hubbard; John and Brenda Scranton; Ann Hopkins; Betsy Baker; Carleen Gunther; Susan Forstmann-Kealy; Caroline Ramsay; Ellen Kerney; the Contessa Elaine and Tom August; Countess Edith Hadik; James P. Lew; Chris Vasiliou; Richard Steiger; Andrula Zinon; Yiota Pappas; Nubia Salguero; Cathy and Stanley Zgaljic; Peter Stassi; Helen and Paul Jacobs; Mr. and Mrs. Phillip Haralambou; Marian S. James; the late Theodore James, Sr.; Tazia James; Joanne, Scott, and Jay James; Debbie Jacobs; Dr. Edmund Weber Jones; Dr. George Broniek; Bill and Barbara Wilhelm; Doug and Jane Hardy; Sarah Hartnett; Bruce and Barbara Georgi; Francis George; Ida Vail; Dorothy and Luke Lueckoff; and Burton's Book Store, Greenport, N.Y.

Shady Hill Gardens, Batavia, Ill.; Jackson & Perkins Co., Medford, Oreg.; W. Atlee Burpee Co., Warminster, Pa.; McCormick & Co., Hunt Valley, Md.; Bluestone Perennials, Madison, Ohio; George W. Park Seed Co., Greenwood, S.C.; Thompson & Morgan, Jackson, N.J.; Caswell & Massey Co. Ltd., New York, N.Y.; Penn Herb Co., Philadelphia, Pa.; Pierre Deux, New York, N.Y.; Tom Thumb Workshops, Chincoteague, Va.; Indiana Botanic Gardens, Hammond, Ind.; Hyponex Corp.; Doyle Lumber, Martinville, Va.; Claire Burke Home Fragrance, Minnetonka, Minn.; Smith & Hawken, Mill Valley, Calif.; Scarborough & Co., Wilton, N.H.; Roses of Yesterday and Today, Watsonville, Calif.; Well Sweep Farm, Port Murray, N.J.; Netherlands Flower Bulk Institute; Robert La Rue Associates.

Further we wish to thank our agent, Mrs. Carleton Cole, and our editor, Pam Hoenig, for their encouragement and enthusiasm.

Introduction

Every summer for years, as the roses in my rose garden passed their prime, I looked at the bonanza of rose petals simply going to waste and thought to myself, "This year I will make potpourri." I would then make half-hearted attempts at finding recipes and instructions here and there, but was always discouraged. The recipes called for such things as *Uva-ursi* leaves, tonka beans, or orris root, things I had never seen and did not know where to buy, let alone had ever heard of. I began to think I would end up on my death bed saying, "Damn! I never made that potpourri!"

As a substitute, I would buy commercially available potpourris, only to be disappointed by their lack of sparkling color and interesting ingredients, and by the fact that their scent rarely lasted more than a month. And that they were so expensive further dampened my enthusiasm for what I have now come to call "dead leaves," potpourri in a cellophane bag.

Then two years ago I installed a planting of lavender as a small hedge in one of my gardens. By summer, the haunting scent of the purple blue flowers filled the air. I realized that I now had not only an endless supply of rose petals, but a substantial supply of lavender as

well. I did know that these two ingredients are basic to potpourri.

In the meantime, I had sunk deeper and deeper into my world of gardening, swaggering around the place in ratty old blue jeans and a pair of hefty Army boots. Friends had begun to complain that I was becoming "insufferably macho." "Now is the time," I thought, "to make potpourri." Not only would I be able to satisfy my curiosity and the challenge afforded, but I could soften my image just a bit.

So I began research and discovered that all I would need to create my own potpourris would be some essential oils, which I would have to locate and buy, some fixative, which I would also have to locate and buy, and all of the different dried materials.

As I investigated further, beyond a scattering of local health food stores, I discovered that there are mail-order houses that offer the oils, fixatives, and all different kinds of dried flowers, berries, and leaves. One house offered dried bachelor's buttons and *Calendula,* another dried lavender, *Artemisia,* and hyssop. I knew these materials could be grown right at home in my own garden, and hence this book, *The Potpourri Gardener,* was born, a how-to guide not only to making your own homemade potpourri, but also to growing and gathering everything you need right in your own garden or in the wild.

I installed a potpourri garden, grew all of the materials described in this book and created the potpourris. I discovered not only the joys and wizardry of making potpourris, but the delight of enjoying and showing off the garden to friends and visitors. I found that children and beagles, in particular, are utterly enchanted and fascinated with a potpourri garden. As they stroll through, they take bits and snippets of this or that herb or scented plant, and smile or bark with delight as they try to identify the scent. So then, my pleasure has been twofold, once in the lovely scented garden, and again in the scented potpourris that perfume the house and that have been given as gifts to so many.

I sincerely hope that the information contained in this book will help you to share in the enthusiasm and delight which has been mine.

How to Use This Book

We will be concerned with three aspects of potpourri:

- How to grow the material necessary for making potpourris
- How to harvest and prepare materials for potpourri use
- How to make potpourri

Before you begin to plant, read chapter 1, "Creating Your Potpourri Garden." Then read through the various encyclopedias in the following chapters, acquainting yourself with the plants suitable for making potpourri, namely those that retain their color, scent, or both when dried; naturally you will not wish to plant all of the cultivars included, for there are far too many for the average garden. Check the U.S.D.A. Hardiness Zone Map opposite to see whether the plants you have chosen are hardy in your location.

Look through the recipes offered in the recipe section (chapter 9) and decide which of the many kinds of potpourris you think you might want to make. Take note of the necessary ingredients, as many of them can be grown in a potpourri garden. Begin to think about what kinds of textures, colors, and scents you like. Also think about your own limitations in terms of time and available garden space.

Then, with these factors in mind, you can start to make your selection of the plants you wish to grow. Remember that spring is the best time to install any garden in most parts of the country, and it is also the best time to plant your potpourri garden.

During late winter, visit your local garden centers and nurseries and inquire whether or not the plants and seeds you wish for your garden will be available. Some plants you want may not be carried in the average nursery or the selection may be limited. For example, although a local nursery may offer rose-scented geraniums, they may not have all of the other scented varieties available. However, there is a mail-order source for a near endless variety of scented geraniums, at very reasonable prices. Avail yourself of these mail-order sources; for your convenience, I have an extensive listing of such sources at the end of the book. Write to them for their catalogues (they are usually free), make your selections, and send in your order.

Once planted (and complete planting and cultivations are included in the encyclopedias), harvest potpourri material for drying throughout the season.

A final word about making potpourri. Please note that the recipes are divided into the four seasons: spring, summer, autumn, and winter (holiday). Some of the spring potpourris call for material that is only available in the summer or fall, such as the soft, fuzzy leaves of betony or the scented, silver foliage of *Santolina* and *Artemisia*. As the seasons progress, dry the material and store it away until you have everything needed for a particular potpourri. Or, in lieu of that, substitute any other kind of suitable material for that which you don't have.

As the seasons change, you will probably want to change the potpourris in your house. No need to throw them out. Pack them in a ziplock plastic bag and store them away until next year. Then, if they've lost a little of their scent, simply sprinkle several drops of the essential oil used in it and shake it around. Close the plastic bag again and let it sit for about a week. The fresh oil will revive the scent infused in the fixative and the potpourri will once again offer a strong scent. If for some reason or other you don't have any essential oil left, or have misplaced it, a few drops of brandy serves the same purpose.

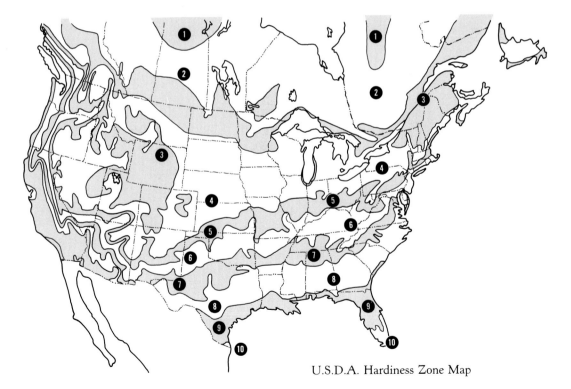

U.S.D.A. Hardiness Zone Map

Creating Your Potpourri Garden

❧

Preceeding page: A potpourri garden can be a treat to the eye at any time during the growing season. The garden is glorious in the fall when chrysanthemums dominate the scheme. *Above:* Employing geometric forms is a traditional way to plan your potpourri garden.

Spring is the best time to install your potpourri garden of herbs, perennials, annuals, shrubs, and roses. Fall is the time to put in the spring-blooming bulbs. Since most of the garden is installed in spring, during the dreary days of late winter plan your garden and decide which plants you wish to grow.

Almost all gardeners, no matter how experienced, think on a grandiose scale when planning a garden. But be advised that you must be realistic about your scheme in terms of how much time you have to spend planting and maintaining it. Start on a small scale, and then, once you have one season's experience under your belt, reevaluate the size of your garden and the amount of time you can devote to it.

Beyond the time element, look over your property with an eye for space. If you have a small plot of ground, naturally, you will have to install a small potpourri garden. If your landscape is well established, at this point you might not be willing to rip up a portion to install a self-contained potpourri garden. In this case, you might wish to plant within the framework of the existing landscape.

If you decide you want a self-contained potpourri garden, there are many options open to you. You can create a formal, rectangular bed somewhere on your property or in the middle of your lawn. An informal potpourri border, located in front of an existing shrub or perennial planting, is another possibility.

If you decide that you want a formal, classic, geometric potpourri garden, there are many possible designs open to you. Perhaps the most popular is a series of four quadrants set in a square, with paths dividing the quadrants and a focal point, such as a birdbath, sundial, or sculpture, in the middle.

If your space is severely limited, you can plant in window boxes or in containers on a deck, balcony, or patio. And you can even grow many potpourri plants indoors on a sunny windowsill.

Regardless of what form you decide upon, plan on making room for a garden bench or seating area somewhere near the garden or planting, where you and your friends can linger and enjoy the heady fresh scents of the herbs and flowers at your leisure.

Locating Your Garden

Whether large or small, the preferred location for a potpourri garden is in full sun, in an area sheltered from the wind. If you do not have an area on your property with full sun, try to plant the garden in the place that gets the most sun each day, as most of the plants will thrive in partial shade, although they won't grow and bloom as profusely. If possible, locate your garden near a window or screened porch so that the fragrances from the planting will scent the house during the summer months and you will be able to see its beauty from inside.

Flat areas are ideal for siting a potpourri garden. However, gentle slopes facing the sun, or even steep hills that can be terraced, are also appropriate.

Garden ornaments such as statuary and birdbaths add focal points to a potpourri garden. Here feverfew grows beside a sundial.

Planning Your Garden

Once you've determined how much time and space you wish to devote to your garden, it is time to plan. It is always a good idea to design a scheme on paper. Measure the space you've selected and outline it on graph paper, using a ratio of one inch to one foot of garden space. If you've decided on a traditional, classic garden, allow space for paths and charming garden statuary, as well as a bench, sundial, birdbath, or sculpture as a focal point. Paths should be at least three feet wide to make them comfortable for walking. Try to plan all the beds so they are no wider than five feet, preferably accessible from both sides. This is to facilitate weeding, harvesting, and maintenance.

You might wish to enclose your garden. If so, make plans now for a fence, wall, or hedge. In addition to setting off the garden, enclosures provide barriers against strong wind, both protecting plantings and ensuring that their scents are not dispelled on a breezy day. Aesthetically, enclosures provide privacy and, thus, an intimate experience for anyone visiting your garden.

If you plan on installing some of the shrubs recommended for potpourri material, you might wish to incorporate them into the enclosure for your garden; if not, it is probably better to install them in other parts of the garden, since most are too large for a basic potpourri garden of herbs and flower material.

Selecting the Plants

Once you've decided upon your scheme, it is time to select the plants you wish to grow.

Here roses are combined with delphiniums in a breathtaking garden display. All are suitable for pot-pourri use.

Read the various encyclopedias and learn which of the flowering plants are herbs, annuals, perennials, and bulbs. Take notes on those you wish to include and jot down their mature height and growth habit. This will help you to determine how much space is needed for each of them.

As you select plants and note them on your plan, keep the following in mind:

• After spring bloom, the foliage of bulbs must be left to ripen if they are to bloom the next spring. It can definitely look messy in the garden as it completes its seasonal cycle. If possible, overplant annuals in the spring-blooming bulb areas.

• If you have designed a border, place tall plants in the back, those of medium height in the middle, and low-growing plants in front.

In a free-standing bed, tall plants belong in the middle, then medium height plants with low-growing plants around the edges. If you are installing a formal, geometric potpourri garden, consider using perennial herbs as a hedge to outline the various forms. *Santolina*, dwarf lavender, and hyssop are all attractive choices.

• Follow the spacing instructions in the encyclopedias carefully. You will be amazed to find that a potpourri garden that looks very sparse when planted will be lush and almost crowded by fall. As with any bed or border, if you have the space, plant at least three of each variety so they can make their own statement visually.

• Since you are planting herbs as well as flowering annuals and perennials, think in terms of foliage contrast. There are so many shades of silver, blue, and green in herbal foliage that you can play them off one another. Textures also vary and can be used to advantage aesthetically. Velvety betony can be placed next to needlelike lavender. Feathery, brilliant green tansy works nicely with the rich, lustrous leaves of lemon verbena. Leaf shapes also afford nice contrast. If you already have some experience growing herbs, this kind of planning may come naturally to you. If this is your first attempt, be patient, for you will make mistakes. By the second year, you will begin to become more familiar with the various colors, shapes, and textures of the plants suitable for potpourri and can transplant to achieve a more pleasing combination.

• Use the annual and perennial flowering plants as color contrast in the garden. Intersperse them among the herbs. Again, you may find the first year that a particular combination doesn't suit you. You can always change it the following year. As a general rule, colors adjacent to one another on the color wheel blend well, those opposite do not.

By combining different colors and textures you can achieve a garden that is not only useful for its scents, but visually striking as well. The lush green hedge makes a distinctive backdrop.

For those who wish to install only a small potpourri garden, either due to lack of time or space, here is a list of plants, the *bare minimum*, which are essential:

Annuals: Bachelor's button *(Centaurea),* pot marigold *(Calendula),* larkspur (annual delphinium), zinnia.
Perennials: Chrysanthemum, peony *(Paeonia),* yarrow *(Achillea),* candytuft *(Iberis).*
Herbs: Lavender *(Lavandula),* lemon verbena *(Aloysia triphylla)* or lemon balm *(Melissa officinalis), Artemisia.*
Roses: A yellow-blooming Floribunda ('Sunsprite') and a red-blooming Floribunda (see chapter 6).
Bulbs: Miniature daffodils, *Muscari* 'Blue Spike'.
Shrubs: Firethorn *(Pyracantha)* for berries, any of the boxwoods *(Buxus)* for green foliage.

This border reveals how beautifully the flower and foliage colors of potpourri plants work together in the garden.

Preparing the Soil

Assuming that you've planned your garden on paper and selected the plants you wish to grow, now it is time to get out into the garden and work. First, transfer your paper plan to the garden site. Measure and then use stakes and string to outline the plot. Within the plot, use more string and stakes to outline areas for the various types of plants.

Prepare the soil to ensure the best growing conditions for your plants. Do this as soon as the ground is workable in the spring, many weeks before installing your garden. Although most of the plants you will use do not require overly rich soil, to the point that some even resent it, some preparation is essential for success. As a general rule, apply a six-inch layer of well-rotted compost or sphagnum peat moss on the top of the bed and dig it in to a depth of one foot. If soil is heavy in clay, work in a large bag of perlite as well.

Purchasing Plants and Seeds

Once the beds are ready, take out the list of plants you want to grow and note which are annual herbs and flowers, which are perennial herbs and flowers, and which are bulbs. You will notice in the various encyclopedias that the purchase of some plants (roses, shrubs, and many perennial herbs and flowering plants) from garden centers or nurseries is recommended. This is because many are difficult or impossible to grow from seed. Follow this ad-

Massed plantings, in this case with daffodils, often work to stunning effect.

for the potpourri garden must be divided every few years, most gardeners are more than willing to share any excess they might have with you.

When you do purchase perennial plants, roses, and shrubs from local sources, look for plants that are strong and have healthy, vigorous new growth, with vibrant leaf color. If disfigured or infested with insects, don't buy it. Plants should also be labeled to make sure you're getting what you want.

Many annual herbs and flowers can be grown from seed. Some must be planted as soon as the soil is workable in the spring, others after all danger of frost has passed. Make sure you follow the instructions on the seed packet when planting. The alternative to planting from seed is to purchase six-packs of individual plants at local nurseries or garden centers.

Planting the Potpourri Garden

Chances are the plants you will be installing will be small and quite tender. For this reason plant in early morning, late afternoon, or on a cloudy day, when strong, direct sun won't wilt or scorch plants.

Carefully remove plants from their pots. Don't try to yank them out or you will disturb the root system. Rather, turn the pot upside down with your hand covering the soil and the stem between your fingers. Tap the pot gently and the plant should fall into your hand. Inspect the root system. If it is thickly tangled, loosen the roots somewhat.

Dig a small hole and set the plant in it with the top of the roots just below soil level. Put a little soil around the roots and water. When the water has drained, fill the rest of the hole

vice carefully, or you will most likely be disappointed with the results of your efforts. If any one or several varieties are not available locally, order from mail-order sources (see "Sources for Planting Material").

Beyond that, you may be able to avail yourself of plants from friends, family, or neighbors who have gardens. Since many plants suitable with soil, pack down gently, and water again. Be sure to water the plant every day until new growth begins.

Taking Care of Your Garden

Because so many of the plants included in a potpourri garden are pest and disease resistant, you will probably not have to deal with these problems. And, because many are also drought resistant, watering, rather than being a daily chore, is usually a weekly chore, and then mainly during prolonged summer drought. To conserve moisture and cut down on weeding and maintenance, apply a mulch to the garden. Cedar or pine chips, to a depth of about three inches, serves this purpose, in addition to looking very attractive. Two bags of this inexpensive material, available at most garden centers and nurseries, is enough to cover a two-hundred-square-foot garden.

TWO

Herbs

Preceding page: Pineapple sage (*Salvia elegans*) not only imparts a lovely scent, it sports stunning, brilliant crimson blossoms.

Dried herbs are an essential ingredient in any potpourri. They offer scent, texture, and the soft gray, blue, and green colors, affording both visual and fragrance versatility. And a stroll through a potpourri garden on a midsummer evening, with the scents of lemon verbena, pineapple sage, the mints, rose-scented geraniums, and others wafting through the still air is pure enchantment.

There are many herbs which you can select for your potpourri garden; however, if space and time are limited, here are those that are essential for scent.

- Lemon verbena
- Lavender
- Rosemary
- A selection of scented geraniums

For texture and color, be sure to plant the following:

- Betony, or lamb's ears, for its velvety, silver foliage
- Any *Artemisia* (southernwood) or santolina for its silver foliage as well as scent
- Sweet woodruff, which is very easy to grow

and adapts to shady conditions, adds deep green color, and the scent of fresh-mown hay to a potpourri creation

Artemisia
Silver King (*A. albula*), Silver Queen (*A. ludoviciana* var. *albula*), Silver Mound (*A. schmidtiana*)

. . .

Half-hardy perennial

The *Artemisia* family is a large one, boasting over two hundred varieties. However, only a few varieties are suitable for potpourri. It was known in France as Armoise and in England and early America as mugwort, and is still used medicinally as well as in perfumes and for culinary flavor.

Although *Artemisia* is used in potpourri for its subtle lemony scent, its silvery foliage and flowers are indispensable in creating visually attractive and interesting potpourris. They are also used in dried flower arrangements and wreaths.

Zones: 5 to 9. Treat as an annual in zone 4 and in the northern stretch of zone 5.

Outdoor planting time: Late spring or fall.

Light: Full sun.

Soil: Poor to ordinary, sandy or gravelly.

Moisture: Water only during extended summer drought, since too much water rots the roots of the plant.

Description: Silver foliage with white seed heads.

Height: 2 to 3 feet.

Growing instructions: Since *Artemisia* requires special conditions to grow from seed, it is best to purchase plants. Set plants about 3 feet apart and divide every three years.

. . .

Use in potpourri: Silver leaves and white seed heads used mainly for color.

Scent: Slightly lemony.

Harvest time: Cut stalks in late summer or early fall, when seed heads are pure white.

Recommended drying method: Hang drying. Before using in potpourri, cut the stalks into pieces about 1 inch in length, since larger pieces tend to cling to each other, not mixing with other ingredients. You might want to cut larger pieces of the white seed head to use as decoration on the top of a potpourri creation.

Basil *(Ocimum basilicum)*

. . .

Annual

This popular culinary herb is also used extensively in potpourri. There are so many interesting varieties to choose from, you might find you want to grow several. There is common sweet basil *(O. basilicum),* lemon basil *(O. basilicum* 'Citriodorum'), purple basil *(O. basilicum* 'Dark Opal'), which has reddish purple leaves and rose-pink flowers, and miniature basil *(O. basilicum* 'Minimum'), just to name a few. Basil is used in potpourri to add zest.

Zones: 3 to 9.

Outdoor planting time: Spring, after all danger of frost.

Light: Full sun.

Dried purple basil *(Ocimum basilicum* 'Dark Opal') adds a deep color to a potpourri.

Soil: Well drained, but moist.

Moisture: Water regularly during growing season.

Description: Attractive bright green or purple leaves with white or rose-colored flowers in late summer or early fall.

Height: 1 to 2½ feet, depending on variety.

Growing instructions: Plant seeds; when seedlings are 3 inches high, thin to 1 foot apart.

. . .

Use in potpourri: Leaves and flowers used for scent as well as their green or purple color.

Scent: Sweet or lemony, depending on variety.

Harvest time: Cut stalks throughout growing season.

Recommended drying method: Hang drying.

stalks in midsummer.

Height: 6-inch-high mat with flower stalks 12 to 18 inches tall.

Growing instructions: Grow from seed or purchase plants. Thin to 18 inches when seedlings are 2 inches tall. Many potpourri gardeners remove the flowering stalks to keep the plant orderly during growing season. Divide every two years.

. . .

Use in potpourri: Leaves are used for silver color and fuzzy texture.

Scent: Negligible.

Harvest time: Pick leaves throughout the season.

Recommended drying method: Strip leaves from stalks and place in baskets and dry in warm, dry place. Store in an airtight container in a cool, dark place until ready to use.

Betony or Lamb's Ears (*Stachys*)

. . .

Hardy perennial

The silvery leaves of lamb's ears are indispensable in visually attractive potpourris.

Zones: 4 to 9.

Outdoor planting time: Late spring or fall.

Light: Prefers full sun, but will grow in partial shade.

Soil: Well drained, ordinary.

Moisture: Water only during prolonged summer drought, as water tends to rot foliage.

Description: Low mat of woolly, silvery white foliage that carries purple flower

Chamomile (*Matricaria chamomilla*)

. . .

German or Hungarian
Half-hardy perennial

Translated from the Greek, *chamomile* means ground apple, so-named because of its apple-like aroma. It is still used to make a relaxing, sleep-inducing tea and as a hair rinse. Shakespeare said of it, "The more it is trodden on, the faster it grows." It is used in potpourri to add a subtle apple scent.

Zones: 5 to 9.

Outdoor planting time: In spring, after all danger of frost.

Light: Prefers full sun, but will grow in partial shade.
Soil: Well-drained, but moist, light soil.
Moisture: Water regularly during growing season.
Description: Matted, bright green foliage with daisylike white flowers in late summer or early fall.
Height: 2 to 4 inches.
Growing instructions: Purchase plants and set 1 foot apart. Divide after three years.

. . .

Use in potpourri: Dried flowers are used for scent and pale yellow color.
Scent: Applelike.
Harvest time: Harvest flowers when they open.
Recommended drying method: Hang drying.

Costmary (*Chrysanthemum balsamita*)

. . .

Hardy perennial

The name *costmary* derives from the Latin *costus,* which means an Oriental plant, and from the Virgin Mary. Early on, the large, flat leaves were used to flavor ale and were called alecost. This plant was also called Bible Leaf because its leaves were used as bookmarks in Bibles. During the Middle Ages and the Renaissance it was scattered on floors to scent rooms. A small amount of costmary will add zest to a potpourri.

Zones: 4 to 9.

Outdoor planting time: Spring, after all danger of frost.
Light: Prefers full sun, but will grow in partial shade.
Soil: Well drained.
Moisture: Water only during prolonged summer drought.
Description: Long, narrow, light green leaves with erect stems which bear yellow flowers in summer.
Height: 2 to 3 feet.
Growing instructions: Grow from seed or purchase plants. Thin to 2 feet apart when seedlings are 2 inches tall.

. . .

Use in potpourri: Leaves used sparingly for scent.
Scent: Peppery combination of mint, lemon, and balsam.
Harvest time: Pick leaves just before the plant flowers.
Recommended drying method: Hang drying.

Feverfew (*Chrysanthemum parthenium*)

. . .

Hardy perennial

An attractive plant with charming daisylike blooms, which add color and character to a potpourri garden. In cold winter areas it dies to the ground in fall, but resprouts in spring.

Zones: 4 to 9.
Outdoor planting time: Spring, after all danger of frost.
Light: Prefers full sun but tolerates partial

Add color and scent to potpourri with feverfew blossoms.

shade; flowering is less likely, however.
Soil: Well drained.
Moisture: Water only during prolonged summer drought.
Description: Light green leaves with daisylike blossoms on long stems.
Height: 18 to 20 inches.
Growing instructions: Grow from seed or purchase plants. Thin to 2 feet apart when seedlings are 2 inches tall. If conditions are favorable, will self-sow prodigiously. Easy to control by pulling up unwanted plants.

· · ·

Use in potpourri: Flowers add color and scent.

Scent: Similar to costmary, for they are related botanically.
Harvest time: When flowers bloom in midsummer.
Recommended drying method: Hang drying.

Geranium, Scented (*Pelargonium*)

· · ·

Half-hardy perennial

Certainly these are among the potpourri gardener's best friends. However, like their cousins, bedding geraniums, they are not hardy

One of the scores of varieties of scented geraniums useful in potpourri. This one is 'Pungent Peppermint.'

where winter temperatures drop below 20° F. But northern gardeners can pot them up in the fall, bring them indoors, and winter them over. Or you can take cuttings from established plants in the fall, root them in water, pot them up, and grow them on a windowsill. By spring, they will be large enough to plant outdoors.

Scented geraniums are available in dozens of beguiling scents: rose, lemon verbena, lemon, apricot, pine, chocolate, peppermint, lime, apple, coconut, nutmeg, almond, and many others. They are extremely handsome plants and indispensable in the potpourri garden. Some sport blossoms; however, they are generally undistinguished. There are bedding varieties and others suitable for growing in hanging baskets.

Zones: Hardy only in zones 8 and 9. In zones 4 to 7, winter indoors or treat as an annual.

Outdoor planting time: Spring, after all danger of frost.
Light: Full sun in cool, northern climates; partial shade in the hot climates of the South.
Soil: Not fussy, as long is drainage is adequate.
Moisture: Water during prolonged summer drought.
Description: Fuzzy, medium green leaves on handsome plants.
Height: 1 to 3 feet, depending on variety.
Growing instructions: Purchase plants and set about 2 feet apart. Pinch tips throughout the growing season to encourage bushiness.

. . .

Use in potpourri: Leaves add subtle scent and soft green color.
Scent: Dozens. See introduction above.
Harvest time: Harvest leaves anytime during the season.
Recommended drying method: Hang drying.

Hyssop (*Hyssopus officinalis*)

. . .

Hardy perennial

A valuable herb for potpourri, and adapts well to borders and beds. In ancient times it was used to preserve meat and to scent rooms. The name is derived from the Hebrew *azob*, which means holy plant. During the Middle Ages, every monastery garden included hyssop, as it was believed to remove skin spots. Elizabethans used it to cure everything from coughs to ringing ears. Oil of hyssop is used to flavor

Chartreuse liqueur. It is one of the few herbs that has adapted to the wild throughout the United States.

Zones: 4 to 9. Grows wild throughout the United States.
Outdoor planting time: Spring or fall.
Light: Prefers full sun, but will grow in partial shade.
Soil: Not fussy, but prefers good drainage.
Moisture: Drought resistant, but water during extended summer drought.
Description: Smooth, dark green, woody, evergreen perennial with purple blossoms from mid to late summer through to fall.
Height: 1½ to 2 feet.
Growing instructions: Purchase plants or start from seed. Thin to 18 inches apart when seedlings are 2 inches tall.

. . .

Use in potpourri: Leaves and flowers for scent.
Scent: Subtle licorice.
Harvest time: From late spring through early winter.
Recommended drying method: Hang drying.

Lavender (*Lavandula*)

. . .

Half-hardy perennial

Lavender is probably the most universally popular fragrance used in potpourri, and utterly essential to any potpourri garden. There are many varieties of lavender, however English lavender (*L. angustifolia*) is the easiest to grow, the hardiest, and the most aromatic. French lavender (*L. dentata*) is hardy only to zone 8, while spike lavender (*L. latifolia*) is hardy through zone 6, although the plant is not nearly as aromatic or attractive as English lavender.

Throughout history, lavender has been a very popular herb, used as a cure for fits, hoarseness, and aching joints. Its lovely scent captivated Tudor England, to the point that today, in the south of France, as well as in England, lavender is an important agricultural commodity, sought by manufacturers of soaps, perfumes, and other scented luxury items worldwide.

A dooryard garden of English lavender (*Lavandula angustifolia*), indispensable to many potpourri creations.

Zones: 6 to 9, although may survive if well protected during winter in the southern stretches of zone 5. Farther north, treat as an annual.

Outdoor planting time: Spring or fall.

Light: Prefers full sun, but will grow in partial shade.

Soil: Sandy soil with good drainage is ideal.

Moisture: Water only during extended summer drought.

Description: Narrow, 2-inch-long, silvery gray leaves with tiny lavender, rose, or white flowers, depending on the variety.

Height: L. angustifolia grows to 4 feet, depending on variety. Lower growing, more manageable varieties include 'Hidcote' (12 inches), 'Munstead' (18 inches), and 'Compacta' (10 inches).

Growing instructions: Purchase plants or start from seed anytime from late spring to midsummer and transplant to garden. Thin to 1 foot apart when seedlings are 2 inches tall. If plant becomes leggy after flowering, cut back.

· · ·

Use in potpourri: Leaves and flowers used for scent and color. Seeds can be used for scent as well.

Scent: Lavender.

Harvest time: Leaves throughout the season, flowers in midsummer to late fall when they begin to show color, but have not completely opened. Oils are most concentrated if you harvest at noon.

Recommended drying method: Hang drying. Since flower heads add color as well as scent to potpourri, you will probably want to store them separately from the foliage. Remove the heads first and store in an airtight container in a cool, dark place until ready to use. Strip the leaves from the stalks and store in the same manner.

Lemon Balm *(Melissa officinalis)*

· · ·

Hardy perennial

Hardy and easily grown throughout the United States, lemon balm is a member of the mint family. The great botanist Linnaeus named it *melissa,* the Greek word for bee, for honeybees flock to it. If lemon verbena plants are not available in your area, lemon balm is a reasonable, although not nearly as fragrant, substitute.

Zones: 4 to 9.

Outdoor planting time: Spring, summer, or fall.

Light: Prefers full sun, but tolerates semishade. I have a stand that grows under a dense yew tree, deeply shaded, although plants in full sun grow more vigorously here.

Soil: Rich.

Moisture: Water regularly during prolonged summer drought.

Description: Light green leaves with tiny white flowers in late summer.

Height: 2 to 3 feet.

Growing instructions: Purchase plants and set about 2 feet apart. Plants spread vigorously. Occasional cutting back promotes new leaf growth and helps retain bushiness. Divide every year to create more plants.

. . .

Use in potpourri: Leaves offer scent and green color. Flowers offer scent.
Scent: Lemon.
Harvest time: Anytime during the growing season; however, for potpourri purposes, it is best to harvest just before flowering when leaves are at their most fragrant.
Recommended drying method: Hang drying.

Lemon Verbena (*Aloysia triphylla*)

. . .

Annual

Another of the potpourri gardener's best friends and quite probably the all-time favorite potpourri and sachet scent. However, like scented geraniums, they are not hardy where winter temperatures drop below 10° to 15° F. But northern gardeners can pot them up in the fall, bring them indoors, and winter them over, although dry conditions cause them to drop their foliage and sometimes die. It is best to purchase new plants each spring, treating lemon verbena as an annual. Native to South America, lemon verbena was introduced to North America by the Spanish explorers during the sixteenth century.

Zones: 8 and 9, although may thrive with protection in southern parts of zone 7. In zones 4 to 7, winter over indoors or treat as an annual.
Outdoor planting time: In spring, after all danger of frost.
Light: Prefers full sun.
Soil: Well drained, moderately fertile.

Moisture: Water regularly, particularly during prolonged summer drought.
Description: Narrow, deep green leaves, 3 to 4 inches long, with small white flower clusters at branch tips in late summer.
Height: 1 to 3 feet.
Growing instructions: Purchase young plants and set about 2 feet apart. Pinch plant tips to promote bushiness.

. . .

Use in potpourri: Leaves and flowers.
Scent: Lemon.
Harvest time: Gather leaves from midsummer through frost, although the plant is most highly scented just before its blossoms open.
Recommended drying method: Hang drying.

Marjoram (*Origanum majorana*)

. . .

Half-hardy perennial

Marjoram, related to oregano, is a member of the mint family. Commonly called sweet marjoram, during the Middle Ages it was used to sweeten the indoor smell of houses, as well as in perfumes, sachets, and potpourri.

Zones: Hardy in zones 8 and 9. Further north, treat as an annual.
Outdoor planting time: In spring, after all danger of frost.
Light: Prefers full sun.
Soil: Slightly alkaline.
Moisture: Water lightly during season, particularly during extended summer drought.

Description: Small oval leaves, light green on top, gray-green underneath, covered with soft fuzz. White to lilac flowers form in tight clusters at tops of stems in midsummer.

Height: 1 to 2 feet.

Growing instructions: Purchase plants or sow seeds outdoors. Thin to 1 foot apart when seedlings are 2 inches tall. To encourage bushiness late in the season, cut back after flowering.

. . .

Use in potpourri: Leaves and flowers add scent and silver color.

Scent: Marjoram.

Harvest time: Throughout the season, but leaves are most aromatic just before flowering.

Recommended drying method: Hang drying.

Mint (*Mentha*)

. . .

Hardy perennial

There are many varieties of mint, but some are not appropriate for potpourri. Spearmint (*M. spicata*), for example, overpowers any potpourri, making it smell like chewing gum. Pennyroyal (*M. pulegium*) also has a very strong peppermint scent that will dominate any mixture. The most useful mints for potpourri are those with delicate fruity aromas, such as pineapple (*M. suaveolens* 'Variegata'), apple (*M. suaveolens*), orange bergamot (*M. citrata*), and golden mint (*M. gentilis* 'Variegata').

Zones: 4 to 9.

Outdoor planting time: Throughout the growing season, but spring is best.

Light: Prefers full sun, but will grow in partial shade and sometimes in dense shade.

Soil: Not fussy.

Moisture: Drought resistant, but water regularly during extended summer drought.

Description: Bright green or variegated leaves with insignificant white or purple flowers, depending on variety, from early to late summer.

Height: From 1 to 3 feet, depending on variety.

Growing instructions: Purchase plants, but be advised that all the mints grow rampantly. To prevent them taking over your potpourri garden, you must contain them. To do this, sink either construction flues (available at lumber yards) or large plastic containers into the ground and set the plants in them. In this way, the underground runners, which spread and create new plants, will be restricted, preventing them from becoming a nuisance.

. . .

Use in potpourri: Leaves and flowers.

Scent: Depending on the variety, mint, lemon, apple, pineapple, orange.

Harvest time: Throughout summer and fall.

Recommended drying method: Hang drying.

A variety of mints are set off by colorful dianthus in this potpourri garden.

Rosemary (*Rosmarinus officinalis*)

. . .

Half-hardy perennial

This is another of the indispensable potpourri herbs that is rich in history, legend, and lore. The color of its blue flower is said to have come from the Virgin Mary, who placed her cloak on a rosemary bush, bringing the color of the sky to it. It also is believed that the Virgin hid behind a rosemary bush during her flight to Egypt. Shakespeare said in *Hamlet* that rosemary is the symbol of remembrance and fidelity. It has been used for just about everything, from inducing sleep to healing wounds, restoring hair and youth, and easing headaches. In medieval France it was burned as incense in hospitals to ward off the spread of disease and used everywhere as a strewing herb to scent rooms.

There are many varieties available, all appropriate for a potpourri garden; however, the most readily available are 'Albus,' which has white flowers, and 'Collingwood Ingram,' which grows from 2 to 3 feet high. A smaller variety, 'Prostratus,' grows only to 2 feet, and adapts well to hanging baskets and small garden spaces.

Zones: 7 to 9. Further north, pot up in fall and winter over indoors or treat as an annual.

Outdoor planting time: Spring, after all danger of frost.

Light: Prefers full sun.

Soil: Light, well drained.

Moisture: Drought resistant but water regularly during extended summer drought.

Description: Light green needlelike leaves

A large rosemary bush makes a wonderful backdrop for sweet woodruff, tarragon, and the other potpourri herbs.

with blue, purple, or white flowers, depending on the variety.

Height: 2 to 4 feet, depending on the variety.

Growing instructions: Purchase plants and set 2 feet apart.

. . .

Use in potpourri: Leaves and flowers for scent and texture.

Scent: Sweet, pinelike.

Harvest time: Throughout the season, but scent is heaviest just before bloom time in late summer.

Recommended drying method: Hang drying.

Sage (Salvia)

· · ·

Hardy or half-hardy perennial

Sage is another herb, useful in potpourri, with a long and fascinating history. The word *salvia* derives from the Latin *salvere,* which means "to save," implying curative powers. During the Middle Ages, it was thought to cure baldness and impart wisdom. The word *sage* means one with wisdom. There are many species of sage, but the most readily available is common garden sage *(S. officinalis),* with oval, gray-green leaves. *S. aurea* has variegated green and gold leaves and pineapple sage *(S. elegans)* has light green leaves that impart a strong pineapple aroma.

Zones: 4 to 9, except pineapple sage *(S. elegans)* which is hardy only in zones 8 and 9. Farther north, either pot up and winter over indoors or treat as an annual.
Outdoor planting time: Spring, after all danger of frost.
Light: Prefers full sun.
Soil: Poor, well drained.
Moisture: Drought resistant.
Description: Fuzzy, oval, gray-green, yellow-green, or deep green leaves, with purple, red, or rose flowers, depending on the variety.
Height: 1 to 5 feet, depending on the variety.
Growing instructions: Purchase plants or grow from seed outdoors. Thin to 2 feet apart when seedlings are 2 inches tall.

· · ·

Use in potpourri: Leaves and flowers, for scent and texture.

Scent: Sage or pineapple, depending on the variety.
Harvest time: Throughout the growing season; however, the bright red pineapple sage blossoms should be harvested during its bloom period in late summer and early fall.
Recommended drying method: Hang drying.

Southernwood (Artemisia abrotanum)

· · ·

Hardy perennial

Southernwood is a very attractive plant, useful in any part of the garden as a shrub, hedge, or background plant. In France it is still used as a moth repellent, and from the Middle Ages through the nineteenth century parishioners would bring quantities of it to church because it prevented drowsiness. It has always been thought of as an aphrodisiac and has been called "Lad's Love" and "Maiden's Ruin." The most common variety available is lemon scented. If you are lucky, and they are worth seeking out, you may find a source for the tangerine- and camphor-scented varieties.

Zones: 4 to 9.
Outdoor planting time: Spring, after all danger of frost.
Light: Prefers full sun.
Soil: Well drained, average.
Moisture: Drought resistant, but water regularly during extended summer drought.
Description: Lacy, gray-green leaves with feathery texture, bearing pale yellow

Tansy (*left*), artemisia (*lower right*), and lemon verbena (*upper right*) create a subtle but eye-catching contrast in color and texture, as well as impart lovely scents.

flowers in mid to late summer.

Height: 2 to 4 feet.

Growing instructions: Purchase plants and set 3 feet apart. Trim each year to keep plant tidy. Divide every three to four years.

. . .

Use in potpourri: Leaves and flowers for soft texture and scent.

Scent: Subtle lemon, tangerine, or camphor, depending on the variety.

Harvest time: Harvest leaves anytime, the flowers just before they open.

Recommended drying method: Hang drying.

Tansy (*Tanacetum vulgare*)

. . .

Hardy perennial

Through history, tansy has been used primarily as an insect repellent and a medicine for everything from the plague to colic. At one time, cakes made of tansy were given to winning athletes. Although the herb is still effective in warding off moths in closets and chests, its strong camphor scent can overpower a potpourri. However, the delicate little yellow blossoms dry well, retain their color, and add just a touch of zest to a potpourri. Use it sparingly in your creations.

Zones: 4 to 9.
Outdoor planting time: Spring, after all danger of frost.
Light: Prefers full sun.
Soil: Ordinary, but well drained.
Moisture: Drought resistant, but water regularly during prolonged summer drought.
Description: Fernlike dark green leaves with petite, button-type, yellow flowers in midsummer.
Height: 2 to 4 feet.
Growing instructions: Purchase plants and set 2 feet apart.

· · ·

Use in potpourri: Flowers add subtle scent and color; leaves, however, will overpower a potpourri.
Scent: Mild camphor.
Harvest time: When flowers bloom in midsummer.
Recommended drying method: Hang dry, then remove flowers and store in an airtight container in a cool, dark place until ready to use. As long as you have the leaves, why not thresh them, fashion them into a sachet, and use them in closets and chests to ward off moths?

꧁꧂

Tarragon (*Artemisia dracunculus*)

· · ·

Hardy perennial

There are two varieties of tarragon available: French and Russian. Because of its stronger, more flavorful aroma and taste, French tarragon is preferred for both culinary and potpourri usage. Tarragon was known to the ancient Greeks, but only reached central Europe in the sixteenth century, when the French named it *esdragon,* meaning dragon, because the plant's roots resembled a mass of serpents.

Zones: 5 to 7. Does not thrive in warmer climates: Tarragon needs a chill period during winter.
Outdoor planting time: Spring, after all danger of frost.
Light: Full sun or partial shade.
Soil: Well drained.
Moisture: Drought resistant, but water regularly during prolonged summer drought.
Description: Narrow, shiny, deep green leaves with occasional insignificant flowers.
Height: 1 to 2 feet.
Growing instructions: Purchase plants and set 2 feet apart. Mulch heavily during winter in colder regions. To keep plant vigorous, divide every three years.

· · ·

Use in potpourri: Leaves for scent and texture.
Scent: Strong licorice with a touch of vanilla.
Harvest time: Early summer, before flowering, is when the aroma is the

Thyme adds not only fragrance to potpourri, but the green of its leaves and its lilac-colored blossoms.

strongest; however, you can harvest all season.

Recommended drying method: Hang drying.

Thyme (*Thymus*)

. . .

Hardy perennial

Thyme is another essential herb for the potpourri gardener. The name derives from the Greek *thymon*, which means courage, for the Greeks felt that the herb imparted strength and courage to those who partook of it. It is known that Virgil grew thyme, as he felt his bees made the most flavorful honey from the nectar of this herb. During the Middle Ages, women embroidered scarves depicting bees taking the nectar from thyme branches and presented them to brave knights.

Thyme is very easy to grow, with some varieties that are hardy throughout the country, and attractive in the garden. There are over fifty varieties of thyme; many gardeners actually specialize in the growing of it.

Zones: 4 to 9.
Outdoor planting time: Spring, after all
danger of frost, summer, or fall.
Light: Full sun or partial shade.
Soil: Well drained, ordinary.
Moisture: Drought resistant, but water
regularly during prolonged summer
drought.
Description: Silver, yellow-green, or green
leaves with pink, white, or rose blooms
from early to late summer, depending on
the variety.
Height: From 3 to 18 inches, depending on
the variety.
Growing instructions: Purchase plants or
grow from seed, although germination is
slow. Thin when seedlings are 1 inch tall.
Low-growing varieties are perfect for rock
gardens or the front of a border. Taller
growing varieties are handsome in borders
and beds. Plant low-growing varieties
(Mother-of-Thyme, so called to
distinguish them from taller varieties) 8
inches apart, taller varieties 12 to 18
inches apart.

. . .

Use in potpourri: Leaves and flowers for
aroma, color, and texture.
Scent: Lemon (*T. citriodorus:* 'Aureaus' has
green and yellow leaves, 'Argenteus' has
silver leaves), coconut (*T. praecox*
'Coccineus'), caraway (*T. herba-barona*),
or rose (*T. serpyllum roseum*, the hardiest
of all).
Harvest time: From early summer through
fall.
Recommended drying method: Hang drying.

Woodruff or Sweet Woodruff
(*Galium odoratum*)

. . .

Hardy perennial

Another treasured potpourri herb, sweet
woodruff is still used in Europe to flavor May
wine. During the Middle Ages it was used
medicinally as a cure for heart, liver, and stom-
ach problems. Teutonic knights wore it in their
helmets to promote success in battle, while
Queen Elizabeth I offered favorite people a
sprig of this herb. It is still used commercially
in perfumes and body lotions.

Zones: 4 to 9.
Outdoor planting time: Spring, after all
danger of frost.
Light: Prefers partial to deep shade.
Soil: Well drained, rich.
Moisture: Drought resistant, but water
regularly during prolonged summer
drought.
Description: Pointed, deep green leaves with
tiny, white clusters of flowers at stem
ends in early summer.
Height: 8 to 12 inches.
Growing instructions: Purchase plants and
set 12 inches apart. Since it is drought
resistant, sweet woodruff is an ideal
ground cover under large shade trees,
where, because of the trees' surface roots,
moisture is at a premium. However, it can
run rampant in a border or bed.

. . .

Use in potpourri: Leaves and flowers for
scent and color.
Scent: Woodsy, with vanilla overtones.
Harvest time: Throughout the season.
Recommended drying method: Hang drying.

THREE

Annuals

Preceding page: A planting of annuals—here, celosia and dusty miller—are attractive in the garden and can be dried for potpourri use.

Annuals live for only one growing season. They bloom and when the flowers turn to seed, they have completed their growing cycle. To extend their blooming season, "deadhead," that is, remove all spent flowers during the season. Frost kills the plants, so they must be replanted every year.

Most annuals are easy to grow, require little care during the season, and, for the most part, are pest and disease free. They also offer a lovely display in the garden as well as an abundance of cutting material for bouquets in the house. The potpourri gardener can rejoice, for these carefree plants provide a bonanza of material for drying.

If you only have the space or the time to grow a few varieties of annuals for potpourri use, the most indispensable are:

- bachelor's button
- calendula (pot marigold)
- larkspur
- zinnia

If space and time allow for more, the other varieties recommended offer a wider color range and thus more possibilities for attractive potpourri combinations.

The encyclopedia below includes those annuals most useful in potpourri. However, don't limit yourself to these easy-to-grow and recommended varieties. If you have other favorites, experiment with them, try drying them, and if you think they will be attractive in your potpourri, by all means use them.

Bachelor's Button or Cornflower
(*Centaurea cyanus*)

· · ·

Among the easiest of all annuals to grow, its blue flowers retain a remarkable brilliance when dried, making them essential in a potpourri garden.

Zones: 3 to 9.
Outdoor planting time: Seeds resist cold, so sow about six weeks before it is time to set out tomatoes in your area.
Light: Prefers full sun, but tolerates some shade.

Pot marigolds (yellow) and bachelor's buttons (purple) grow in tandem. Both are indispensable to potpourri.

Soil: Ordinary.

Moisture: Resists drought, but water regularly during prolonged summer drought.

Description: Thistlelike, pink, white, blue, or purple flowers with closed heads on silver-green foliage.

Height: Standard variety grows to 2½ feet and can look unkempt unless supported. Dwarf variety grows to about 1½ feet and is more manageable in most gardens.

Growing instructions: When seedlings are 2 inches tall, thin to 8 to 12 inches apart. Deadhead old blooms to lengthen display;

otherwise, plants tend to bloom themselves to death and become unsightly by midsummer.

. . .

Use in potpourri: Flower heads, particularly the blue varieties, retain their brightness and add color.

Scent: Negligible.

Harvest time: Throughout flowering season, from early summer through frost.

Recommended drying method: Hang drying.

Cockscomb (*Celosia cristata*)

. . .

Akin to the everlastings, cockscomb adds not only brilliant color, but also provides interesting texture in a potpourri.

Zones: 3 to 9.

Outdoor planting time: Easy to grow. Sow seeds outdoors after all danger of frost.

Light: Prefers full sun.

Soil: Light and rich.

Moisture: Drought resistant, but water regularly during extended summer drought.

Description: Medium green foliage with feathery, velvetlike flowers in brilliant red, orange, apricot, yellow, or fuchsia.

Height: 9 inches to 2 feet.

Growing instructions: If grown from seed, thin to 1 foot apart when plants are 4 inches high. If you purchase six-packs from garden centers or nurseries, set plants about 1 foot apart. The only pest you may have to deal with is red spider. If this pest strikes, hose down the planting daily during midsummer. Many consider *Celosia* garish, and the colors are very overwhelming in a bed or border, so you may not want to set your plants amid an established bed or border.

. . .

Use in potpourri: Flowers retain brilliance and are used for color. Reds are particularly useful for holiday potpourris.
Scent: Negligible.
Harvest time: Throughout flowering season, from early summer through frost.
Recommended drying method: Hang drying.

Everlastings

. . .

This name is given to a group of flowering annuals which dry particularly well and can be added to potpourri. Very often they are sold in flower shops, nurseries, and even supermarkets in the fall; however, you can grow almost all of them from seed. Several that you might wish to plant in your potpourri garden are globe amaranth, strawflower (*Helichrysum*), and statice.

Zones: 3 to 9.
Outdoor planting time: Spring, after all danger of frost.
Light: Prefers full sun, but tolerates partial shade.
Soil: Well drained, average.
Moisture: Drought resistant, but water regularly during prolonged summer drought.
Description: Brilliant or pastel-colored flowers of pink, gold, red, rose, yellow, purple, salmon, white, or silver-blue,

depending on variety.
Height: 1 to 2 feet, depending on variety.
Growing instructions: For early bloom, start seed indoors under lights eight weeks before last frost (do not cover seeds as they need light to germinate) or sow directly outdoors after all danger of frost. Thin to 1 foot apart.

. . .

Use in potpourri: Blossoms add color.
Scent: None.
Harvest time: Throughout flowering season from midsummer through frost.
Recommended drying method: Hang drying.

Larkspur (*Delphinium ajacis*)

. . .

Annual delphinium or larkspur is much easier to grow than perennial delphinium and offers similar pink, white, purple, or blue blossoms.

Zones: 3 to 8.
Outdoor planting time: Seeds resist cold, so sow as early in spring as ground can be worked.
Light: Prefers full sun.
Soil: Moderately rich and well drained.
Moisture: Resists drought, but water regularly during prolonged summer drought.
Description: Spikes of blue, red, white, pink, or purple blossoms on medium green foliage.
Height: 3 to 4 feet.
Growing instructions: Sow in early spring; larkspur seeds will not germinate in warm weather. Thin to 1 foot apart when

Annual blue and white larkspur dry well and will naturalize in your garden, prodigiously self-sowing.

seedlings are 2 inches tall. Use as background for borders, or as specimen plants.

. . .

Use in potpourri: Flowers, particularly blue and purple, add color.

Scent: Negligible.

Harvest time: During bloom period in midsummer.

Recommended drying method: Hang drying.

Marigold (Tagetes)

· · ·

These easy-to-grow, popular annuals retain their yellow, gold, and orange colors quite well, although not as well as pot marigolds (see page 45). If you must choose between the two, select pot marigolds.

Zones: 3 to 9.
Outdoor planting time: After all danger of frost.
Light: Prefers full sun, but will tolerate partial shade.
Soil: Ordinary.
Moisture: Drought resistant, but water regularly during prolonged summer drought. Plants will tell you when they need water by wilting.
Description: Yellow, orange, gold, or rust blossoms on handsome, deep green foliage. Depending on the variety, flowers range in diameter from 1 to 5 inches.
Height: Depending on the variety, from 6 inches to 4 feet.
Growing instructions: Very easy to grow. Start plants indoors under lights four weeks before last frost or sow seeds where you want them to grow. Thin dwarf varieties to around 8 inches apart, taller varieties to 18 to 24 inches apart when seedlings are 1 inch tall.

· · ·

Use in potpourri: Flowers, which retain brilliance when dried, are used for color. Smaller flowering varieties can be used whole, petals of larger flowering varieties can be added separately.
Scent: Unpleasant when fresh, negligible when dried.

Harvest time: Throughout growing season.
Recommended drying method: Hang drying.

Nasturtium or Indian Cress (Tropaeolum)

· · ·

The brilliant oranges, reds, maroons, and rusts of dried nasturtiums add festive fall touches to potpourris. The plants are easy to grow and drought resistant. And, as a bonus, both leaves and flowers are edible; they'll add a peppery touch to salads.

Zones: 3 to 9.
Outdoor planting time: After all danger of frost.
Light: Prefers full sun, but tolerates partial shade.
Soil: Ordinary.
Moisture: Drought resistant, but water regularly during prolonged summer drought.
Description: Funnel-shaped yellow, orange, or red flowers on pea green leaves. Standard and climbing varieties.
Height: 6 inches for standard prostrate varieties, up to 5 feet for climbers.
Growing instructions: If soil is too rich, foliage will be lush, but flowers will be few. Soak seeds overnight before sowing to hasten germination. Thin to 6 inches when seedlings are 4 inches high.

· · ·

Use in potpourri: Flowers retain brilliance and are used for color.
Scent: Peppery when fresh, negligible when dry.

Harvest time: Throughout flowering season, from midsummer to frost.
Recommended drying method: Hang drying.

Pansy (*Viola wittrockiana*)

· · ·

The beloved pansy, readily available at garden centers and nurseries in the early spring, is ideal for planting in a window box. Select blue, purple, or yellow varieties for potpourri drying.

Zones: 3 to 9.
Outdoor planting time: Since pansies resist cold temperatures, plant outdoors in window boxes or beds about six weeks before it is time to set out tomatoes in your area.
Light: Full sun or partial shade.
Soil: Ordinary.
Moisture: Water regularly throughout season.
Description: Blue, purple, yellow, apricot, orange, mahogany, or white blooms on deep green foliage.
Height: 6 to 8 inches.
Growing instructions: Purchase plants or sow from seed. When plants are 1 inch tall, thin to 8 to 12 inches apart. Deadhead spent blooms to lengthen display. If plants become rangy, pinch back to encourage new foliage and bloom.

· · ·

Use in potpourri: Blossoms retain their brightness and add color.
Scent: Negligible.
Harvest time: Throughout flowering season,

from early spring through frost.
Recommended drying method: Best dried in silica gel or by air drying.

If space is at a premium, there are many plants suitable for potpourri that can be grown in window boxes, such as the pansies here, which dry well and retain their color.

Pinks, Carnations, or Sweet William
(Dianthus)

. . .

Before cloves from the East Indies were readily available throughout Europe and North America, the scent of *Dianthus* was used as a substitute in potpourris fashioned to refresh rooms.

Zones: 3 to 9.

Outdoor planting time: After all danger of frost.

Light: Prefers full sun, but tolerates partial shade.

Soil: Well drained, average.

Moisture: Drought resistant, but water regularly during prolonged summer drought.

Description: Brilliant-colored flowers of scarlet, salmon, white, yellow, pink, or crimson on attractive silver-green foliage.

Height: Pinks range from 8 to 12 inches, carnations from 12 to 36 inches, and sweet William to 24 inches.

Growing instructions: For early bloom, start seed indoors under lights eight weeks before last frost or sow directly outdoors. Thin to 6 to 8 inches apart when seedlings are 1 inch tall. Harvest flowers or deadhead regularly to prolong bloom. Use in beds, borders, planters, window boxes, and for cutting.

. . .

Use in potpourri: Blossoms add color and scent.

Scent: Clove.

Harvest time: Throughout flowering season, from midsummer through frost.

Recommended drying method: Hang drying.

The all-time favorite, sweet William, a member of the *Dianthus* family, adds a clove scent to a potpourri.

Pot Marigold (Calendula officinalis)

. . .

When dried, pot marigolds retain their brilliant orange, yellow, gold, or apricot colors better than any other plant. This flowering annual is a must in any potpourri garden. The flowers are edible and can be used to add attractive touches to salads.

Zones: 3 to 9.

Outdoor planting time: Calendula seeds resist early spring cold. Sow where you want them to grow about four weeks before it is time to set out tomatoes in your area.

Light: Prefers full sun.

Soil: Ordinary.

Moisture: Resists drought, but water regularly during prolonged summer drought.

Description: Upright plants with fleshy, medium green foliage. Yellow, gold, orange, or apricot blooms on upright, brittle, stiff stems.

Height: 12 to 18 inches.

Growing instructions: Easy to grow. Deadhead spent blossoms regularly to lengthen bloom. Thin to 9 inches apart when seedlings are 1½ inches tall.

· · ·

Use in potpourri: Blossoms are added for color.

Scent: Negligible.

Harvest time: Throughout flowering season, from early summer through frost.

Recommended drying method: Hang drying.

Salvia or Sage

· · ·

The red varieties provide color useful in holiday potpourris.

Zones: 3 to 9.

Outdoor planting time: After all danger of frost.

Light: Full sun or partial shade.

Soil: Well drained, ordinary.

Moisture: Drought resistant, but water regularly during prolonged summer drought.

Description: Brilliant red or blue spikes of flowers on lush, dark green foliage.

Height: 1½ to 4 feet, depending on variety.

Growing instructions: Colors are so vivid it

Salvia 'Victoria' is a regal plant in the potpourri garden and keeps its lovely blue color when dried.

is difficult to use them effectively in borders. Sow seed indoors under lights eight weeks before last frost, then set outdoors. Or purchase plants in six-packs from garden centers or nurseries. Set 8 inches apart. When plants are 3 to 4 inches high, pinch tops to encourage branching and, thus, more flowers.

· · ·

Use in potpourri: Flowers retain brilliance when dried and are used for color.
Scent: Sagelike when fresh, negligible when dried.
Harvest time: Throughout flowering season, from midsummer through frost.
Recommended drying method: Hang drying.

Zinnia

. . .

Another easy-to-grow, popular annual that offers many pastel shades not available in other plants. Try installing a mixture to make the most of the color versatility of this plant.

Zones: 3 to 9.
Outdoor planting time: After all danger of frost.
Light: Prefers full sun, but will tolerate partial shade.
Soil: Ordinary.

Moisture: Drought resistant, but water regularly during prolonged summer drought. Plants will tell you when they need water by wilting.
Description: Blossoms are all colors of the rainbow except blue, set on fleshy, deep green foliage. Depending on variety, flowers range in diameter from 1 to 7 inches.
Height: 6 inches to 4 feet, depending on variety.
Growing instructions: Sow seeds where you want them to grow. Thin dwarf plants to 9 inches apart, taller growing varieties to 2 feet when seedlings are 2 inches tall.

. . .

Use in potpourri: Flowers, which retain brilliance when dried, are used for color. Dwarf flowers can be used whole; petals of larger flowering varieties can be used as well.
Scent: Negligible.
Harvest time: Throughout flowering season, from midsummer through frost.
Recommended drying method: Hang drying.

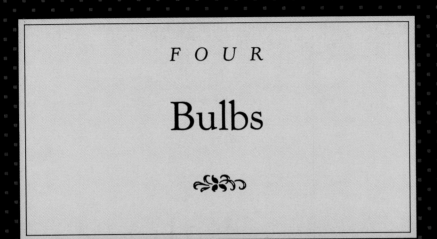

FOUR

Bulbs

Preceding page: Many fall- and summer-blooming bulbs, such as this tiger lily, have blooms that dry well and retain color.

Many spring blooming bulbs are suitable for potpourri and add charming touches to your creations. With the exception of lilies, all are planted in the fall. If it is possible to single out varieties that are the most utile in making potpourris, plant any of the miniature daffodils and *Muscari* 'Blue Spike.'

Crocus

. . .

For potpourri purposes, select only 'Giant Yellow' and purple 'The Sultan.' White 'Jeanne d'Arc,' lilac 'Queen of the Blues,' and 'Striped Beauty' do not hold color well. Species crocus, those that bloom very early in the season, are very small and are not worth drying.

Zones: 3 to 10.
Outdoor planting time: September to December.
Light: Full sun or partial shade.
Soil: Ordinary, with good drainage.
Moisture: Water only if there is a late

These golden yellow crocus are among the first blossoms of spring that you can gather for drying.

winter or early spring drought, since corms are dormant during summer.

Description: Cup-shaped blossoms over green and silver needlelike foliage.

Height: 6 inches.

Growing instructions: Set bulbs 4 inches apart. Each year, just before bloom, scratch a handful of 5-10-5 fertilizer into the soil around the planting. Crocuses multiply rapidly, so when planting becomes overgrown, dig up in fall, separate, and replant for more drying material.

. . .

Use in potpourri: For brilliant color.

Scent: None.

Harvest time: At peak of bloom, in early spring.

Recommended drying method: Best dried in silica gel or by air drying.

Daffodil and Jonquil (*Narcissus*)

. . .

The larger varieties of daffodils can be used to decorate the tops of spring potpourris. The miniature varieties are charming mixed with other ingredients.

Zones: 4 to 10.

Outdoor planting time: September to December.

Light: Full sun or partial shade.

Soil: Ordinary, with good drainage.

Moisture: Water only if there is a late winter or early spring drought, since bulbs are dormant during summer.

Description: Blossoms in various shades of yellow, orange, or white, and combinations thereof, over jade green straplike foliage.

Height: 4 to 18 inches, depending on variety.

Growing instructions: Set standard bulbs 6 inches apart, minis 4 inches apart. Each year, just before bloom, scratch a handful of 5-10-5 fertilizer into the soil around the planting. Deadhead after bloom, but allow foliage to ripen until it dries completely, as nutrients in leaves return to the bulb and nourish next year's bloom. Daffodils multiply rapidly, so when planting becomes overgrown and blooms become sparse, dig up in fall, separate, and replant for more drying material.

. . .

Use in potpourri: Large varieties for brilliant color; miniatures for color and charm.

Scent: None.

Harvest Time: At peak of bloom, in mid-spring.

Recommended drying method: Best dried in silica gel or by air drying.

Glory-of-the-Snow (*Chionodoxa*)

. . .

Although you will have to use a lot of blossoms to make an impact with their blue color, even a few, sprinkled through a primarily yellow spring potpourri, adds a sparkling touch.

Zones: 3 to 10, but grow best in cooler climates.

Outdoor planting time: September to December.

The blue flowers of early-blooming glory-of-the-snow dry well and add sparkle to spring creations.

Light: Full sun or partial shade.
Soil: Ordinary, with good drainage.
Moisture: Water only if there is a late winter or early spring drought, since bulbs are dormant during summer.

Description: Intense, star-shaped blue blossoms with white eye, over straplike foliage.
Height: 6 inches.
Growing instructions: Set bulbs 3 inches

apart. It is not necessary to fertilize or deadhead. When plantings become crowded, dig up in fall, divide, and replant bulbs.

. . .

Use in potpourri: For sprinklings of deep blue color.
Scent: None.
Harvest time: At peak of bloom, in early spring.
Recommended drying method: Dry individual blossoms in silica gel or air dry.

Grape Hyacinth (*Muscari*)

. . .

Of all the bulbs, *Muscari* is the one that holds not only its color, but much of its scent as well. In the garden, 'Blue Spike' is a more attractive plant, because it does not send up messy foliage in the fall prior to next season's bloom, as do other varieties of *Muscari*.

Zones: 2 to 10.
Outdoor planting time: September to December.
Light: Full sun or partial shade.
Soil: Ordinary, with good drainage.
Moisture: Water only if there is a late winter or early spring drought, since bulbs are dormant during summer.
Description: Clusters of purple blossoms resembling bunches of grapes over straplike, somewhat messy foliage. 'Blue Spike' is a feathery variety.
Height: 6 inches.
Growing instructions: Set bulbs 3 inches apart. Each year, just before bloom,

scratch a handful of 5-10-5 fertilizer into the soil around the planting. Grape hyacinths multiply rapidly, so when planting becomes overgrown, dig up in fall, separate, and replant for more drying material.

. . .

Use in potpourri: Dried blooms for color and texture.
Scent: Slight grape aroma.
Harvest time: At peak of bloom, in midspring.
Recommended drying method: Best dried in silica gel or by air drying.

Hyacinth (*Hyacinthus*)

. . .

Select blue, pink, and purple hyacinths. Other colors do not dry well. After you harvest, remove individual petals from the stalk and dry separately.

Zones: 4 to 10.
Outdoor planting time: September to December.
Light: Full sun or partial shade.
Soil: Ordinary, with good drainage.
Moisture: Water only if there is a late winter or early spring drought, since bulbs are dormant during summer.
Description: Columnar spikes of flowerlets over jade green, straplike foliage.
Height: 8 to 12 inches.
Growing instructions: Set bulbs 6 inches apart. Each year, just before bloom, scratch a handful of 5-10-5 fertilizer into the soil around the planting. Stiffness of

Hyacinth flowerets add bold color and a slight scent that reminisces of spring.

ing a beguiling touch to a spring potpourri.

Zones: 3 to 8.
Outdoor planting time: September to December.
Light: Full sun or partial shade.
Soil: Ordinary, with good drainage.
Moisture: Water only if there is a late winter or early spring drought, since bulbs are dormant during summer.

Delicate *Iris reticulata* dries to a deep purple and imparts a light violetlike scent.

bloom loosens up after first year of bloom. Deadhead after bloom, but allow foliage to ripen until it dries completely, as nutrients in leaves return to the bulb and nourish next year's bloom.

. . .

Use in potpourri: For bright color.
Scent: Slight aroma.
Harvest time: At peak of bloom, in midspring.
Recommended drying method: Best dried in silica gel or by air drying.

Iris reticulata and I. danfordiae

. . .

These charming small early spring iris in pur-ple (*I. reticulata*) and yellow (*I. danfordiae*) retain their shape and color when dried, add-

Description: Miniature irislike bloom over insignificant foliage.
Height: 6 to 8 inches.
Growing instructions: Set bulbs 4 inches apart. Each year, just before bloom, scratch a handful of 5-10-5 fertilizer into the soil around the planting.

. . .

Use in potpourri: For delicate texture and color.
Scent: Violetlike.
Harvest time: At peak of bloom, in early spring.
Recommended drying method: Best dried in silica gel or by air drying.

Lily (*Lilium*)

. . .

There are so many varieties of lilies, it is difficult to give recommendations for drying; however, I have found that the hybrid lilies, which grow from 2 to 4 feet and are available in a rainbow of colors, dry satisfactorily. The pastel shades, in particular, retain their delicate color when dried in silica gel. *L. speciosum* ('Rubrum'), Orientals, and Aurelian hybrids do not dry well.

Zones: 3 to 10, depending on the variety.
Outdoor planting time: Spring or fall.
Light: Full sun or partial shade.
Soil: Rich, with very good drainage.

Preceeding page: The petals of most lilies, like the 'Golden Splendor' pictured here, dry well and add splashes of color.

Moisture: Water throughout season, particularly during periods of summer drought.
Description: Trumpet-shaped blossoms in a rainbow of colors on spikes of fleshy, deep green foliage.
Height: 18 inches to 7 feet.
Growing instructions: Before planting, enrich soil with rotted manure, compost (one quart per square foot), or 5-10-5 fertilizer (½ cup per square foot). Set bulbs 6 to 8 inches apart. Deadhead after bloom, but allow foliage to ripen until it dries completely, as nutrients in leaves return to the bulb and nourish next year's bloom.

. . .

Use in potpourri: Dried whole flowers are good for decorating the top of a summer potpourri. Dried petals offer interesting colors for mixing.
Scent: None.
Harvest time: At peak of bloom, from June to September, depending on variety.
Recommended drying method: Best dried in silica gel or by air drying.

Tulip (*Tulipa*)

. . .

There are so many varieties of tulips to choose from, it is difficult to single any out. However, the small species tulips, which bloom early in the spring, do dry well. *T. tarda* is one that holds its yellow and white color nicely. Petals of larger varieties should be removed and dried individually. Lavender, purple, and yellow petals hold their color. White does not, and red and orange turn very dark. Some pale pink tulips petals also retain their color.

Zones: 3 to 7. Climate in zones 8 to 10 is not cold enough during winter to provide chill period necessary for tulips to grow.

Outdoor planting time: September to December.

Light: Full sun or partial shade.

Soil: Ordinary, with good drainage.

Moisture: Water only if there is a late winter or early spring drought, since bulbs are dormant during summer and fall.

Description: Turban-shaped blooms in every color of the rainbow, from tiny miniatures to large Darwin hybrids, over fleshy, jade green foliage.

The petals of these hybrid Darwin tulips will dry well, their bright colors making excellent accents in potpourri.

Species tulips, such as this *Tulipa tarda,* also retain their color.

Height: From 6 to 36 inches.

Growing instructions: Set standard bulbs 6 inches apart, species bulbs 4 inches. Each year, just before bloom, scratch a handful of 5-10-5 fertilizer into the soil around the planting. Deadhead after bloom, but allow foliage to ripen until it dries completely, as nutrients in leaves return to bulb and nourish next year's bloom. Many tulip varieties tend to peter out after two or three years of bloom, particularly the Darwins and lily-flowering varieties. Early-blooming species and Darwin hybrids tend to offer longest life.

· · ·

Use in potpourri: Dried petals add color.

Scent: None.

Harvest time: At peak of bloom, from early to late spring, depending on variety.

Recommended drying method: Dry individual blossoms of smaller varieties and individual petals of larger varieties in silica gel or by air drying.

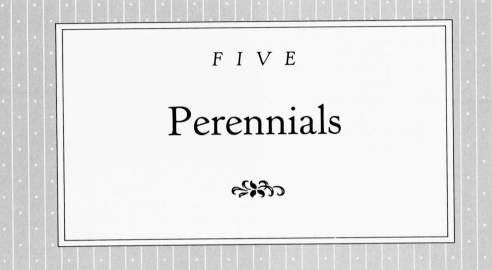

F I V E

Perennials

There are thousands of varieties of perennials that grow in North America. Many sport blossoms that dry well and retain their color, making them suitable for potpourris. However, the following short list includes easy-to-grow cultivars that lend special touches to potpourri, either because of their scent, rich color, or texture. With the exception of delphiniums, all are relatively pest and disease free.

As with annuals and any other type of flowering material, if you already have a selection of perennials growing in your garden, experiment with drying the flowers to see if they retain their color and texture. There is no reason why you can't use any flower that dries well in your creations.

If time and space are limited, chrysanthemums, which bloom in the fall, are the most essential of all the perennials in creating potpourris. Beyond that peony (*Paeonia*), yarrow (*Achillea*), and candytuft (*Iberis*) are all very useful. If delphiniums are particularly problematic in your area, grow annual larkspur instead, since they both provide almost the same colors of blue and purple flowers when dried.

Astilbe

· · ·

Astilbe retains its featherlike texture when dried, adding an engaging aspect to any potpourri.

Zones: 5 to 9.
Outdoor planting time: In spring, after all danger of frost, or in fall.
Light: Prefers partial shade, but may bloom in deep shade.
Soil: Moderately fertile.
Moisture: Moderately moist.
Description: Feathery blossoms in red, pink, peach, or cream on stalks bloom above lush, deep green foliage.
Height: 1 to 2 feet.
Growing instructions: Purchase plants and set about 1 foot apart. Avoid planting under maple or beech trees, as they have shallow surface roots that absorb all the moisture from the soil. Divide every three years to keep plant vigorous.

· · ·

Use in potpourri: Dried blossoms are used for soft color and interesting texture.

Scent: Negligible.
Harvest time: In June and July, when flowers are at peak.
Recommended drying method: Hang drying.

Candytuft (*Iberis*)

· · ·

Candytuft is an easy-to-grow, pest- and disease-resistant plant that remains attractive through the winter because of its evergreen foliage. In a flower bed or border it blends well with the blues of early spring bulbs and the more brilliant-colored tulips.

Zones: 3 to 9.
Outdoor planting time: In spring, after all danger of frost, or in fall.
Light: Full sun or partial shade.
Soil: Well drained and moderately fertile.
Moisture: Moderately moist.
Description: Clusters of white flowers on 1-foot stalks above deep evergreen foliage.
Height: 12 inches.
Growing instructions: Purchase plants and set about 1 foot apart. Divide every three

Spring-blooming candytuft is one of the few white flowers that dries without browning.

years to keep plant vigorous.

· · ·

Use in potpourri: One of the few white
flowers that dries a true white.
Scent: Negligible.
Harvest time: When in bloom, early to
midspring.
Recommended drying method: Hang drying.

Chrysanthemum

· · ·

What would the fall garden look like without
the blaze of color afforded by chrysanthemums? And what would a fall potpourri look
like without these same vivid colors to brighten
them up? Pretty bleak, I'm afraid. Of all the
perennials, chrysanthemums are the most useful in potpourri.

Zones: 5 to 9.
Outdoor planting time: In spring, after all
danger of frost, or in late summer or fall,
when pots are available at garden centers
and nurseries.
Light: Prefers full sun.
Soil: Moderately fertile.
Moisture: Drought resistant, but water
regularly during prolonged summer
drought.
Description: Profusion of rich purple,
maroon, orange, yellow, gold, white, or
lavender blossoms on handsome medium
green foliage.
Height: From 1 to 3 feet, depending on
variety.
Growing instructions: Purchase plants and
set 18 inches apart. If planted in spring,

A basket of cut chrysanthemums and other potpourri material ready to hang dry.

pinch buds once a week until July 4 to
promote bushiness and greater profusion
of flowers. To keep plant vigorous, at
least every other spring, dig plant, discard
woody center, divide, and plant young
side shoots individually.

· · ·

Use in potpourri: Dried flowers for color.
Scent: Negligible.
Harvest time: During peak bloom time, from
September through and beyond frost.
Recommended drying method: Hang drying.

Coralbells (*Heuchera sanguinea*)

· · ·

Easy to grow and drought resistant, coralbells sport sprays of brilliant rose flowers that dry well and add a special touch to summer potpourris.

Although tiny, dried coralbell blossoms are enchanting in potpourri.

Zones: 3 to 9.
Outdoor planting time: In spring, after all danger of frost.
Light: Prefers full sun.
Soil: Well drained and moderately fertile.
Moisture: Moderately moist.
Description: Clusters of white, red, or rose flowers on tall stalks above feathery foliage.
Height: 18 to 36 inches.
Growing instructions: Purchase plants and set about 1 foot apart. Divide every three years to keep plant vigorous.

· · ·

Use in potpourri: Dried flowers are used for color and texture.
Scent: Negligible.
Harvest time: June and July, at peak bloom time.
Recommended drying method: Hang drying.

Delphinium

· · ·

Although they can be difficult to grow in some parts of the country, they are worth a try, because the flowers of delphiniums dry to brilliant shades of blue and purple. 'Bluebird' is a particularly lovely shade of medium blue.

Zones: 3 to 10.
Outdoor planting time: In spring, after all danger of frost.
Light: Prefers full sun, but tolerates partial shade.
Soil: Very rich.
Moisture: Moderate throughout season.
Description: Towering flowering spikes of

The stately delphiniums retain their blue brilliance when dried. In the garden they usually require some sort of staking.

blue, purple, pink, white, or combinations thereof over medium green foliage.

Height: From 3 to 7 feet, depending on variety and growing conditions.

Growing instructions: Delphiniums grow perennially in the Pacific Northwest. In other parts of the country it is best to either purchase year-old plants each year or grow them as biennials. To do this, plant seeds each spring, nurture during the summer and fall, and mulch heavily during the winter. Then set plants in permanent position the following spring, spacing them 2 feet apart. Often plants survive two or three years, but this depends on local conditions, and winter cold.

. . .

Use in potpourri: Blossoms are used for color.

Scent: Negligible.

Harvest time: In June, at peak bloom time. Often, if spent blooms are removed in June, delphiniums will bloom again in the fall, affording more potpourri material.

Recommended drying method: Hang drying.

Peony (*Paeonia*)

. . .

Because they are somewhat more complicated to plant and nurture, more detailed instructions on growing peonies are included for this entry. However, once installed, they are virtually indestructible and will reward you with a great deal of dried petal material for your potpourris for years to come. After your peonies have grown and begin to bloom you will probably notice black ants crawling around on the buds. Do not worry as they are harmless, merely attracted by sweet secretions on the plant.

Zones: 2 to 8.

Outdoor planting time: August to October in most parts of the country.

Light: Prefers full sun, but tolerates partial shade.

Soil: Well drained, rich.

Lavish peonies not only add color to a potpourri but a subtle, haunting fragrance as well.

Moisture: Water regularly but particularly during prolonged drought periods.

Description: Large, pink, red, white, or cream blossoms on handsome, shiny foliage. For potpourri purposes, select only pink or red varieties; the whites and creams turn an ugly brown when dried.

Height: 3 to 5 feet, depending on variety.

Growing instructions: Purchase plants and dig a hole about 1½ feet deep and 1½ feet across. Fortify the soil removed with substantial amounts of rotted manure or compost (1 quart per plant) or 5-10-5 fertilizer (1 cup per plant). Place the peony plant in the hole and fill with fortified soil so that the buds or "eyes" on the fleshy roots are between 1 and 1½ inches below the soil's surface. These "eyes" are easy to spot, as they are creamy white with a touch of pink. Take a ruler with you to the garden when planting to assure proper depth of planting. If you plant deeper, there will be little or no bloom. If you are installing a peony that was grown in a container, plant it so that the soil surface in the container is even with the surrounding soil surface. Tamp the soil down firmly, water thoroughly, and apply a 2-inch mulch around the plant. If you are planting more than one peony, space about 4 feet apart.

The first year, after the first hard frost, cover the entire plant with about 6 inches of salt hay or other mulching material. You do this to prevent heaving of the plant from alternating freezing and thawing through the winter. After the first year, it is not necessary to mulch during winter. Early the next spring, when shoots begin to emerge from the ground, remove the mulch.

Over-fertilizing is probably the best way to kill a peony, so refrain from feeding until the third year after installation. Then scratch in a handful of 5-10-5 fertilizer in early spring as shoots emerge. Wait another three years or so before feeding again. Deadhead after bloom. After several years, when plants reach maturity, you may find it necessary to stake the flower heads when they are in bloom. After the first killing frost, cut withered foliage to 1½ inches above the soil line.

. . .

Use in potpourri: Petals are used for color and subtle scent.
Scent: Sweet.
Harvest time: When flowers are fully opened, from May to June.
Recommended drying method: Hang drying.

Pinks (*Dianthus*)

. . .

As with the annual variety, pinks were used by Europeans and North Americans for their clove scent before the East Indian spice was readily available.

Zones: 4 to 10
Outdoor planting time: In spring, after all danger of frost, or in fall.
Light: Prefers full sun, but tolerates partial shade.
Soil: Sandy loam.
Moisture: Drought resistant, but water regularly during prolonged summer drought.
Description: Shades of pink, red, apricot, salmon, yellow, or white blossoms over silver-gray foliage.
Height: From 3 to 18 inches, depending on variety.
Growing instructions: Purchase plants and set about 1 foot apart. Divide every three years to keep plant vigorous.

. . .

Use in potpourri: Dried flowers are used for

Old-fashioned pinks impart their delicate clove scent to a potpourri.

color and scent.
Scent: Mild clove.
Harvest time: May through September, depending on variety.
Recommended drying method: Hang drying.

Primrose (Primula)

. . .

These, of the primrose path immortalized by William Shakespeare, are among the earliest blooming of all perennials. Although not essential to a potpourri garden, they are wonderfully charming.

Zones: 5 to 9.
Outdoor planting time: Early spring, as soon as ground is workable.
Light: Partial to deep shade.
Soil: Moderately fertile.
Moisture: Moderately moist.
Description: Clusters of yellow, white, blue, red, purple, pink, gold, or salmon

Early-blooming primroses add a spring touch.

blossoms, and combinations thereof, grow
on stalks above rosettes of bright green
foliage.

Height: 6 to 8 inches.

Growing instructions: In northern areas, *P.
vulgaris* is the most reliable variety.
Pacific hybrids tend to be short-lived, but
plants can be purchased if they do not
survive the winter in your area. Set 8 to
12 inches apart.

. . .

Use in potpourri: Dried blossoms add
brilliant color.

Scent: None.

Harvest time: April and May, when at peak
bloom.

Recommended drying method: Hang drying.

The feathery pink tops of astilbe and the purple
spires of salvia provide a striking contrast of
color, shape, and texture.

Salvia

. . .

Perennial varieties of this old favorite offer
deep blue and purple blossoms that dry well
and are suitable for potpourri.

Zones: Some varieties are hardy in zones 4
to 9, others only in zones 7 to 9. Treat
'Farinacea Victoria' and 'Patens,' the
most readily available, as annuals in zones
4 to 6.

Outdoor planting time: Spring, after all
danger of frost.

Light: Prefers full sun or partial shade.

Soil: Well drained and moderately fertile.

Moisture: Moderately moist.

Description: Clusters of deep blue, indigo, or
purple flowers on medium height stalks
over handsome, deep green foliage.

Height: 18 to 24 inches.

Growing instructions: Purchase plants and
set about 1 foot apart.

. . .

Use in potpourri: Flowers add rich color to a
potpourri.

Scent: Negligible.

Harvest time: In July and August, at peak
bloom time.

Recommended drying method: Hang drying.

Thrift (*Armeria*)

. . .

These tidy plants grow in mounds and are
suitable for rock gardens or at the front of a
border. The deep pink flowers are pom-pom

shaped and add an unusual shape and texture to potpourris.

Zones: 3 to 9.

Outdoor planting time: In spring, after all danger of frost, or in fall.

Light: Prefers full sun.

Soil: Ordinary.

Moisture: Drought resistant once established, but water regularly during summer drought.

Description: Mounds of low-growing silvery green foliage with deep pink or white blossoms.

Height: 1 foot.

Growing instructions: Purchase plants and set about 1 foot apart. Divide every three years to keep plant vigorous. Easy to grow, pest and disease free.

. . .

Use in potpourri: Cloverlike blossoms dry to a soft pink and are used for color and texture.

Scent: Negligible.

Harvest time: Mainly in May and June; however, blooms sporadically throughout season.

Recommended drying method: Hang drying.

Yarrow (*Achillea*)

. . .

Very easy to grow, drought resistant, and pest- and disease-free, yarrow bears brilliant yellow blossoms useful in spring and fall potpourris.

Zones: 3 to 10.

Outdoor planting time: In spring, after all

Yarrow brings sparkle to any garden or potpourri.

danger of frost, through summer and into fall.

Light: Prefers full sun.

Soil: Moderately fertile, but tolerates sandy soil.

Moisture: Drought resistant once established, but water regularly during prolonged summer drought.

Description: Dwarf variety, *A. tomentosa,* suitable for rock gardens, 'Coronation Gold,' and 'Gold Plate' all sport brilliant gold flowers, often too intense for usual gardens, but perfect for a potpourri garden.

Height: A. tomentosa grows from 3 to 6 inches, 'Coronation Gold' and 'Gold Plate' grow from 3 to 4 feet.

Growing instructions: Purchase plants and set low-growing varieties 8 to 12 inches apart, tall varieties 12 to 18 inches. Divide every three years to keep plant vigorous.

· · ·

Use in potpourri: Flowers retain golden brilliance when dried.

Scent: Negligible.

Harvest time: When flowers are fully opened, from May through September, depending on variety.

Recommended drying method: Hang drying.

SIX

Roses

❧❧❧

Preceding page: A sparkling assortment of roses on a drying screen. *Above:* Among the roses suitable for potpourri drying are *(back row, left to right):* 'Peace,' 'Brandy,' and 'Queen Elizabeth'; *(front row, left to right):* 'America,' 'Chrysler Imperial,' and 'Sunsprite.'

Along with lavender, rose petals and whole roses are the two most essential dried ingredients in the making of potpourri. They retain their scent when dried and add lovely color. No potpourri garden is complete without a planting of roses; however, not just any rose variety is appropriate for potpourri use.

Because they are so basic in making potpourri, and because they require more knowledge and care than other plants, detailed instructions for the cultivation and care of roses are included in this section.

SELECTING ROSES FOR POTPOURRI

When you select rose varieties for a potpourri garden, you must choose in a manner different than for the usual rose garden. Although you may be enchanted with the subtle colorations of some of the lovely soft pink, cream, and white varieties, as well as the large bloom of many Hybrid Teas, these are not appropriate for a potpourri garden. Here is what you must keep in mind:

• *Colors that dry well.* As a general rule, red, yellow, and orange roses retain their brilliant colors the best. White roses turn an ugly brown when dried, and pink turns an undistinguished pale pinkish brown.

• *Fragrance.* Many of today's hybrids bear little if any scent. However, some do, so select those that are heavily scented, or choose old-fashioned damask and cabbage rose, all of which have heavy scent.

• *Profusion of bloom.* Since you are growing roses for an abundance of drying material, select varieties that will provide quantity. Although single roses offer much charm, usually they have only a few petals, hardly enough to justify growing them for potpourri purposes. And although you may wish to include some Hybrid Teas for their scent, be sure to include some Floribundas (a division of roses with very profuse bloom) for quantity of petals.

• *Include miniature roses.* Since their mini-blossom can be dried whole, they add captivating touches to potpourris.

If time and space are limited, select one red, one yellow, and one orange-red variety, all Floribundas. If you do not have space for the larger roses, grow the miniatures.

Modern Roses

The most readily available roses are "modern" roses, many of which are suitable for potpourri. Of the hundreds of rose varieties available, the following both offer strong fragrance and retain their color when dried. The various fragrances include those of apple, lemon, clove, cinnamon, true rose, damask, and strawberry. Here are the different types of modern roses available.

The lovely pink and orange-yellow petals of 'Tropicana' retain their color when dried.

HYBRID TEAS AND GRANDIFLORAS

Hybrid Teas are the best known of the moderns, ranging in height from 2½ to 7 feet. Most are 3 to 5 feet tall and produce a single flower on a long stem. Some are fragrant, but many are not. Grandifloras are somewhat larger plants than the Hybrid Teas, the result of a cross between Hybrid Teas and Floribundas. These produce up to a half dozen blooms on each stem. They are vigorous and most are fragrant. The following are recommended for potpourri use.

'Arizona'	Grandiflora	yellow-orange
'Chrysler Imperial'*	Hybrid Tea	red
'Command Performance'	Hybrid Tea	orange
'Crimson Glory'*	Hybrid Tea	red
'Electron'	Hybrid Tea	deep pink
'Fragrant Cloud'*	Hybrid Tea	red-orange
'Granada'*	Hybrid Tea	red and yellow
'Mister Lincoln'	Hybrid Tea	red
'Oklahoma'	Hybrid Tea	red
'Ole'	Grandiflora	red
'Perfume Delight'	Hybrid Tea	cerise
'Sundowner'	Grandiflora	red-orange
'Sutter's Gold'*	Hybrid Tea	yellow
'Tropicana'	Hybrid Tea	red-orange

*These varieties have been given the coveted James Alexander Gamble Award for Fragrant Roses by the American Rose Society.

FLORIBUNDAS

These are small plants, 2 to 4 feet high, extremely vigorous, hardy, and disease resistant. They are usually covered with blossoms smaller than those of Hybrid Tea or Grandiflora blooms. Although most bear some fragrance, yellow 'Sunsprite' is particularly fragrant and retains its bright yellow color when dried. Others that are recommended for potpourri are:

'Anabell'; orange-pink
'Bahia'; coral-orange
'Cathedral'; scarlet, tinted salmon
'City of Belfast'; red
'Europeana'; red
'Eutin'; carmine-red
'Ginger'; scarlet orange
'Gingersnap'; bright orange
'Katherine Loker'; yellow
'Merci'; red
'Orangeade'; orange
'Red Pinocchio'; red
'Spartan'; orange
'Trumpeter'; orange-red

CLIMBERS

Quantity of drying material is what you are looking for when you plan your potpourri garden, so if you have the space, include a Climber in your planting scheme as they offer extravagant bloom. The plants do not attach themselves to surfaces, but must be tied to trellises, fences, or other supports. Many grow to 10 to 12 feet in spread.

'America'; coral
'Blaze'; bright red
'Climbing Chrysler Imperial'; red

The Climber 'America' is fragrant and retains color.

'Climbing Crimson Glory'; red
'Climbing Sutter's Gold'; yellow
'Climbing Tropicana'; red-orange
'Don Juan'; deep red

MINIATURES

These are Lilliputian versions of the larger varieties, growing to a mere 1 foot. If space is a problem, they are the best option. Minis offer tiny blossoms that, when dried, add enchanting touches to potpourri. Select from the following lists. These new Mini Floras (miniature Floribundas) provide the most drying material.

'Classic Sunblaze'; pink (unlike larger
   pink roses, this dries well)
'Orange Sunblaze'; orange
'Red Sunblaze'; bright red
'Royal Sunblaze'; yellow with scarlet
   edges

These traditional miniatures do not offer much drying material per plant, but do offer a wide range of color.

'Beauty Secret'; bright red
'Puppy Love'; multicolored orange, pink,
   and yellow
'Red Cascade'; red
'Red Flush'; red
'Rise 'n Shine'; yellow
'Starina'; orange-red

Old-Fashioned

The old-fashioned cabbage and damask roses, now enjoying a renewed popularity with gardeners, are the most heavily scented of all roses and thus are the best material for potpourri. Bloom is more profuse than most modern roses and they are often disease resistant, entailing less care.

However, they usually are not readily available in local garden centers and nurseries, but there are mail-order houses that specialize in them (see Sources for Planting Material). If you wish to include old-fashioned roses in your potpourri garden, write to these houses at the beginning of the year and ask for their catalogues.

Here is a list of recommended old-fashioned roses that are well suited to drying.

'Charles de Mills'; rose-pink
'Common Moss'; clear pink
'Henri Martin'; clear crimson
'Konigin von Danemark'; pink
'La Reine Victoria'; rose-pink
'La Ville de Bruxelles'; clear pink
'Oskar Cordel'; cherry pink
'Salet'; clear pink
'Tuscany Superb'; dark crimson

BUYING ROSEBUSHES

You can order by mail. There are many reputable suppliers in the United States, and you can almost always count on receiving healthy, vigorous plants (see Sources for Planting Material). Do not order roses from any house that does not offer a replacement guarantee if your plant dies. If you buy from a nursery or garden center, here's what to look for: First check for grade number. Roses are rated #1, #1½, and #2, with #1 the highest rating, and the most expensive grade. Ratings are determined by size and number of canes. Sometimes a #2 grade rosebush will produce excellent roses, although usually it takes a few more years, and more care and feeding than a #1 or #1½. At this point, you would do well to buy only #1 grade roses, this to assure that you have the best possible stock to start out with. Second, check to see if bushes have pale or thick canes. Avoid these—they have been neglected in the nursery. Finally, if there are swellings, strange dark colors, or growths on canes and roots, disease is probably present, so avoid these also.

Time of year to plant: Roses shipped by mail from mail-order nurseries almost always are sent at the proper planting time for your area. Bushes available at nurseries and garden centers are usually also sold and stocked at appropriate planting time.

Where to plant roses: Roses are not fussy about planting sites; however, they do require between four and six hours of sunlight a day, depending on the variety, and prefer the light in the morning. For that reason, a site with an eastern exposure, that is, the side of your house that faces east, is best. A dappled shade southern exposure, full sun northern, or western exposures are also satisfactory. Roses also prefer good drainage and adequate air circulation in order to prevent disease.

PLANTING

To plant all varieties except miniatures, dig a hole about 2 feet across by 1½ feet deep. For miniatures, a 1 foot deep by 1 foot across hole is sufficient. Although roses are not fussy about soil, in any case, whether soil is heavy in clay

Climbing roses, in this case 'Inspiration,' trained on arbors, offer an abundance of petals for potpourri.

or in sand, mix compost, sphagnum moss, or other organic matter in with the soil removed from the hole at a ratio of about 2 parts soil to 1 part additive. If drainage is poor, fill the bottom of the hole with rocks or broken flowerpot shards.

Fashion a cone in the bottom of the hole with some of the soil mixture. If plants are bare root, remove damaged, dried out, or overly long roots with pruning shears. Position the plant in the hole so the roots fall over the cone and the graft (the knobby growth just above the roots) is even or just below soil level in zones 4 and 5 or above soil level in zones 6 to 9. Fill in the soil several inches at a time, tamping it down firmly, until the soil level around the rose is even with the surrounding area. Water thoroughly to remove air pockets in the soil.

Some rosebushes are sold in ready-to-plant boxes or containers. Follow the instructions above for digging and amending the soil. As to the next step, there are two schools of thought. The mail-order nursery's instructions indicate that it is not necessary to remove the paper carton in which the rose is planted as it will simply rot in the ground. Others feel that it is perhaps better to remove the carton and spread the roots out somewhat before planting. The choice is yours. Observe the graft level as above and water thoroughly.

Spacing: Hybrid Teas, Grandifloras, Floribundas, and most old-fashioned roses should be spaced about 2 feet apart from center of bush. Miniatures should be spaced about 1½ feet apart, Climbers along fences should be 6 to 8 feet apart or on trellises about 4 feet apart.

Watering: As a rule, water thoroughly once a week in the morning so that the soil is soaked to a depth of from 1 to 1½ feet deep (about 1 inch of water in an empty coffee can placed nearby). Of course there are many variables, such as humidity, rainfall, and the use of mulch, that may affect this schedule. Use common sense. If there has been substantial rainfall, don't water. If there is summer drought, water. Overhead watering can be employed if you spray your roses regularly with a fungicide. However, it is perhaps best to invest in a soaker hose that seeps water into the ground. These are available at garden centers and nurseries and are quite inexpensive. In this way you will discourage the growth of fungus diseases. If you do water with a regular hose, try to avoid wetting the leaves.

Fertilizing: Products specifically labeled "rose fertilizer" are the best. Ortho sells a product that is a combination fertilizer–systemic pest killer–weed killer. It is available at most garden centers and nurseries. You can save yourself a substantial amount of maintenance work if you use this product. Apply three times during the season according to the instructions on the package.

PESTS AND DISEASES

As a preventive, early in spring, before leaf growth starts, spray bushes with a dormant oil spray (available at garden centers and nurseries) according to manufacturer's instructions. You do this to smother any insects and fungi that may have survived the winter.

Three diseases may attack your plants and affect the quality of the flowers. They are:

- *Rust:* small, powdery, orange spots that appear on the leaves' undersides and spread, ultimately causing the leaves to die. Severe infestation can cause the plant to die.

- *Powdery mildew:* powdery white substance that appears on stems and buds. If allowed to spread it can cause the plant to die.
- *Black spot:* small, black circles that appear first on the underside of a leaf, then spread to the entire plant, weakening it and ultimately causing it to die.

At the first sign of any of the above problems, spray with Funginex, an Ortho product, recommended by the American Rose Society, according to the instructions on the bottle. As a preventive, it is a good idea to apply this spray while the plants are dormant and then once a week during the growing season, particularly after heavy rains. As a preventive measure, water roses only in the morning, so that moisture will evaporate during the day and not leave foliage wet, which leads to disease.

Insects such as aphids, spider mites, and thrips are best controlled with a systemic insect killer. Systemics, which are absorbed into the plant and kill insects on contact, do not leave unsightly residues on the blossoms and buds that you wish to dry. Ortho's three-way fertilizer, weed killer, and systemic poison, applied three times during the season, is an easy way to solve this insect problem. Japanese beetles are best controlled by handpicking. If your infestation is of epidemic proportions, a Japanese beetle trap, available at most garden centers or nurseries, is recommended.

MULCHING

Mulching your roses is a good idea because it helps the plant retain moisture and reduces weed growth. Although there are many different kinds of mulches available, either homemade compost or shredded pine or cedar bark is best for rose plantings.

PRUNING

In the fall, when roses stop blooming and go into dormancy, prune only the tallest branches, to about 3 feet high. This is to prevent winter winds from damaging the plants. If there are any rose hips (seed pods) left on the bushes, cut them off, dry them in a basket, store, and when ready, use them in a holiday potpourri.

Spring is the time for the annual pruning, but different kinds of roses require different pruning techniques. However, if you follow these general rules, you should have success.

- Wait until new growth begins, when buds begin to emerge from canes.
- Prune dead canes to the crown (the crown is the base of the plant). These are brown or black and dried out. Use sharp pruning shears, loppers, or a small saw to do this.
- Prune out frost damaged canes to healthy wood, which is white or light green all the way through the cane.
- Make all pruning cuts at an angle about ⅓ inch above a bud that faces away from the center of the bush.
- Open the center of the bush, that is, prune out thin twigs and stems near the middle. This is particularly important with Floribunda varieties.
- Prune out suckers emerging from below the graft, the knobby growth at the base of the plant. These grow from root stock and will not produce blooms true to the variety you have planted.

Climber roses can be trained to create a canopy of color.

- Thin the bush to 4 to 7 canes, each at least as thick as a pencil. For a more abundant supply of rose petals for drying, prune them to 2 feet. Flowers will be smaller, but there will be more of them.
- When finished, apply Elmer's glue or shellac to all exposed cuts to prevent moisture evaporation and insect infestation.

Pruning Climbers

Climbers require a few special techniques. Most form flowering laterals, that is, side shoots from the main branches. In spring, cut these back to 3 to 6 inches with three or four buds on each. During the summer remove faded flowers to force new blooms. So-called ramblers that bloom only in June should have all two-year-old canes cut to their source after flowering.

WINTER PROTECTION

In colder areas of the country, where temperatures fall regularly below zero, winter protection of bushes is necessary. Wait until after a killing frost (15° to 20° F), bring in some soil, and mound it up around the trunk of the bush to a height of 6 or 7 inches. In spring, wait until the weather has warmed up and new growth commences before removing the earth mound.

CUTTING FOR POTPOURRI

Cut roses for potpourri drying whenever they are in bloom, all during the season. When you harvest, always cut to just above a five-point leaf, as opposed to a three-point leaf. New flowering branches will generally not grow from above three-point leaves. Cut in the morning, after the dew has evaporated; that is when oils are most intensely fragrant. Do not water roses the day you will be gathering material.

DRYING FOR POTPOURRI

You will not only want to dry rose petals for potpourri use, but buds as well. The best way to dry whole miniature or standard rosebuds is to use the silica gel or oven or microwave drying methods. Individual petals can be air dried on screens or oven dried. Rose material is particularly susceptible to insect infestation, so after drying, be sure to follow the advice in the drying chapter on storing material with moth balls.

SEVEN

Shrubs

❧❦❧

Preceding page: You can even gather potpourri material from shrubs in borders or foundation plantings, including many varieties of azaleas.

᠅

Although you may have known that berries of various shrubs make attractive additions to a potpourri, you probably have never thought of the flowers and leaves as being usable. Since there are no flowers that dry green, leaves of some evergreen (broad-leaved) shrubs can provide that color. Many flowering shrubs also offer blossoms that dry well. As always, don't be afraid to experiment with drying any flowers that bloom on your shrubs. You may find that you already have many of the plants listed below. If not, they are readily available at garden centers and nurseries.

If time and space are limited, select easy-to-grow firethorn for berries as they produce an abundance of red or orange fruit. For green foliage, any of the boxwoods is an excellent choice. For blossoms, evergreen azaleas produce a bounty for drying.

᠅

Azalea (Deciduous) ('Exbury,' 'Ghent,' 'Mollis')

. . .

The spectacular blossoms of the deciduous azaleas (that is, those that lose their leaves during winter) dry well and add a range of pastel and brilliant colors to the potpourri palette. They are easily grown, readily available, and provide quantities of drying material.

Zones: 4 to 8.
Outdoor planting time: Spring or fall is best, but will survive summer planting or transplanting.
Light: Full sun or partial shade.
Soil: Rich, slightly acid.
Moisture: Water regularly, particularly during prolonged summer drought.
Description: Spectacular cluster blooms in brilliant red, purple, orange, yellow, pink, salmon, coral, white, or combinations thereof. All are suitable for potpourri except white. Foliage is undistinguished.
Height: 3 to 8 feet, depending on variety.
Growing instructions: Space 6 feet apart. Feed every spring with an acid fertilizer

The blossoms of deciduous azaleas dry well and subtly color a spring potpourri.

commercially available fungus spray, such as Captan, according to manufacturer's instructions.

. . .

Use in potpourri: Dried flowers are used for color.
Scent: None.
Harvest time: In late spring at bloom time.
Recommended drying method: Dry individual blossoms in silica gel or on drying screens.

Azalea (Evergreen) and Rhododendron

. . .

The evergreen azalea, and its sister, rhododendron, also provide a wealth of potpourri material at bloom time. You should be able to harvest several quarts of blossoms from even the youngest plant. As they mature, more and more material will be available to you.

Zones: 3 to 10, depending on variety.
Outdoor planting time: Spring or fall.
Light: Full sun or partial shade.
Soil: Prefers rich soil on acid side.
Moisture: Water regularly, particularly during prolonged summer drought. Plant will tell you if it needs water by wilting.
Description: The full range of colors in large and small clusters, a near endless variety. Deep green or fleshy bronze foliage is *not* suitable for potpourri drying.
Height: From 1 to 50 feet, depending on variety.
Growing instructions: Space evergreen azaleas 4 feet apart and rhododendrons 6 to 10 feet apart, depending on the variety. Feed every spring with an acid fertilizer

such as Miracid, according to manufacturer's instructions. For more abundant bloom the following year, remove spent flower heads remaining on plant. In damp climates, foliage often hosts mildew during the summer. This will not harm the plant but can be unsightly. If that bothers you, apply any

such as Miracid, according to manufacturer's instructions.

. . .

Use in potpourri: Red, pink, salmon, and
purple evergreen azalea blossoms dry well
and retain color. White does not.
Scent: None.
Harvest time: Late spring when in bloom.
Recommended drying method: Dry individual
blossoms in silica gel or on drying screens.

Boxwood *(Buxus)*
Common *(B. sempervirens)*
Japanese or Korean *(B. microphylla)*

. . .

The small green leaves of these species dry
well and retain a deep green color. They thrive
in areas too cold for the popular English boxwood.

Zones: 5 to 10.
Outdoor planting time: Spring or fall.
Light: Full sun or partial shade.
Soil: Average, loamy soil.
Moisture: Water regularly, particularly
during prolonged summer drought.
Description: Attractive, bushy plants with
small, round-tipped, deep green leaves.
Height: 1 to 5 feet, depending on variety.
Growing instructions: Set 6 feet apart. Feed
every spring with an acid fertilizer such
as Miracid, according to manufacturer's
instructions.

. . .

Use in potpourri: Leaves dry well and retain
deep green color.
Scent: None.

Harvest time: Any time during the year.
Recommended drying method: Strip fresh
leaves from stems, place in basket and dry
naturally in a cool, dry place. Every few
days mix leaves around. Drying should
take about a week.

Camellia *(C. japonica* or *C. sasanqua)*

. . .

Camellias are much hardier than generally
thought. Although most people think they grow
only in the South, they can thrive even in
protected areas of zone 6, although a very severe winter may kill all foliage. In zone 7,
where I live, my camellia is now 8 feet tall
and covered with hundreds of lovely pink
blossoms in late April.

Zones: 7 to 10.
Outdoor planting time: Spring or fall.
Light: For best blooming, plant in partial
shade, although plant will survive in full
sun. However, strong sunlight will burn
and brown blossoms, making them
unattractive for potpourri.
Soil: Requires rich loam, so fortify at
planting time with substantial quantities
of rotted compost or sphagnum moss, at a
ratio of about 1 part additive to 1 part
soil.
Moisture: Water regularly, particularly
during prolonged summer drought.
Description: Spectacular blooms in pink,
white, red, or combinations thereof, set
on handsome deep green foliage.
However, for drying only pink and red
are suitable.
Height: 5 to 30 feet, depending on variety.

Growing instructions: Set 6 to 10 feet apart. Feed every spring with an acid fertilizer such as Miracid, according to manufacturer's instructions.

. . .

Use in potpourri: Whole dried flowers are effective in decorating tops of potpourris.
Scent: None.
Harvest time: Late winter to early spring, depending on area.
Recommended drying method: Silica gel.

Euonymous

. . .

One of the most utile evergreen shrubs for the landscape, it is often used as a screen or hedge. The leaves dry well and add a touch of green to a potpourri. Some varieties sport berries in the fall and winter, which also can be used in winter potpourris.

The variegated leaves and bright berries of euonymous add colorful textures.

Zones: 6 to 9. Check locally for varieties hardy in zone 5.
Outdoor planting time: Spring, after all danger of frost, or in fall.
Light: Full sun to deep shade.
Soil: Ordinary.
Moisture: Drought resistant, but water regularly during prolonged summer drought.
Description: Pointed, variegated or deep green leaves, from 1 to 4 inches long, depending on variety.
Height: 3 to 12 feet, depending on variety.
Growing instructions: Purchase plants or take cuttings from established plants and root in sand, being careful to keep constantly moist. Plant 3 to 6 feet apart, depending on variety.

. . .

Use in potpourri: Leaves and berries for color.
Scent: None.
Harvest time: Throughout the season.
Recommended drying method: Hang dry branches or screen dry individual leaves.

Firethorn *(Pyracantha coccinea)*

. . .

Easy to grow and disease resistant, you can grow firethorn as a shrub or espalier it against a fence or the house. Buckets of orange or red berries will be available for drying when the plant matures.

Zones: 6 to 10.
Outdoor planting time: Spring or fall.

Light: Prefers full sun but will thrive in
  partial shade.
Soil: Ordinary.
Moisture: Drought resistant once
  established, but water regularly during
  summer drought.
Description: Deep green foliage, evergreen to
  zone 6, with small white flowers that
  produce showy red or orange berries in

The bright orange berries of firethorn are an
ideal complement to dried chrysanthemum blossoms in fall potpourris.

fall and winter.
Height: Can grow to 20 feet, but can be
  kept in bounds by pruning.
Growing instructions: Set 6 feet apart. Feed
  every spring with an acid fertilizer such
  as Miracid, according to manufacturer's
  instructions.

. . .

Use in potpourri: Berries add color to fall
  and winter creations, leaves retain green
  when dried.
Scent: None.
Harvest time: In fall when berries form.
Recommended drying method: Pick berries,
  place in basket in a dry place, and allow
  to dry naturally. Every few days mix
  berries around. Drying takes about three
  weeks.

Forsythia

. . .

The blossoms of this old-fashioned spring
standby dry well and retain their bright yellow
color. Avoid weeping varieties as they require
annual pruning to keep them under control
once established. Select upright varieties such
as 'Linwood Gold.'

Zones: 5 to 9, but 'Northern Lights' can be
  grown in zones 3 and 4.
Outdoor planting time: Spring or fall.
Light: Full sun or partial shade.
Soil: Ordinary.
Moisture: Drought resistant once
  established, but water regularly during
  prolonged summer drought.
Description: Small, yellow blossoms in early

spring before shrub leafs out. Medium green foliage thereafter.

Height: From 6 to 8 feet, depending on variety.

Growing instructions: Set 6 feet apart. Prune only after bloom rather than early in spring for the most profuse display the next season.

. . .

Use in potpourri: Flowers dry well and retain color.

Scent: None.

Harvest time: Very early spring when in bloom.

Recommended drying method: Hang drying or water drying.

Heather (*Calluna vulgaris*) and Heath (*Erica*)

. . .

The culture and appearance of these two are very similar, except that heath blooms in early spring and heather blooms in summer. Heath will not bloom unless it has full sun, whereas heather will bloom in partial shade as well as sun. Both are suitable for potpourri.

Zones: 4 to 10.

Outdoor planting time: Spring or fall.

Light: Full sun or partial shade.

Soil: Light, sandy, acid soil that is not rich.

If the soil is too rich, the plants will

Heath and heather foliage and blossoms dry well and add interesting texture to holiday potpourris.

become leggy and die.

Moisture: Water regularly, particularly during prolonged summer drought.

Description: Very small blossoms on showy spikes 6 to 8 inches long. Most varieties are purple; however, some are red and white. Leaves are minute, green turning bronze in fall in some varieties.

Height: From 6 inches to 3 feet, depending on variety.

Growing instructions: Set 3 feet apart. Feed every spring with an acid fertilizer such as Miracid, according to manufacturer's instructions. Cut back spent flowers after bloom to encourage new, flower-bearing shoots.

. . .

Use in potpourri: Flowers dry well and retain color.

Scent: None.

Harvest time: Late spring and early summer when in bloom.

Recommended drying method: Hang drying.

Holly *(Ilex)*

. . .

In order for holly to produce berries, you must install two plants, one male and one female. This is to ensure cross-pollination.

Zones: (See individual species.)

Outdoor planting time: Late spring.

Light: Prefers full sun.

Soil: Sandy loam.

Moisture: Water regularly, particularly during prolonged summer drought.

Description: (See individual species.)

Height: (See individual species.)

Its brilliant berries and deep green leaves make holly a festive addition.

Growing instructions: Set 6 to 10 feet apart. Feed every spring with an acid fertilizer such as Miracid, according to manufacturer's instructions.

. . .

Use in potpourri: Berries add color to fall and winter potpourris.

Scent: None.

Harvest time: Late fall through winter.

Recommended drying method: Pick berries,

place in a basket in a dry place, and allow to dry naturally. Every few days mix berries around. Drying takes about three weeks.

American (*I. opaca*)

Grow in northern areas of the country where English holly does not survive winters.

Zones: 5 to 10.
Description: Spiny, lustrous, dark green leaves with brilliant red berries in fall and winter.
Height: Can grow to 50 feet, but can be kept in bounds by pruning.

Chinese (*I. cornuta*)

Zones: 6 to 10.
Description: Shiny, deep green leaves with bright red berries that last through the winter.
Height: To 9 feet.

English (*I. aquifolium*)

Zones: 7 and 8.
Description: Glossy green foliage, with some varieties sporting blue-green foliage, and brilliant red, white, or orange berries.
Height: Can grow to 40 feet, but can be kept in bounds by pruning.

Common lilac *(left)* and the deep purple Persian lilac *(right)* can be hang dried for potpourri use.

Lilac (*Syringa*)

· · ·

There are many lilac hybrids available that grow to manageable height. Persian lilac, with deep purple blooms, grows to only 6 feet and dries particularly well. If you wish to include lilac in your potpourris, select this cultivar.

Although other varieties are lovely, many do not dry well and others grow too tall for the average home landscape. For more profuse bloom the following year, deadhead any flower heads left on the bush after bloom.

Zones: 3 to 9.
Outdoor planting time: Spring or fall.
Light: Full sun or partial shade.
Soil: Prefers fertile, well-drained soil.
Moisture: Drought resistant once established.
Description: Clusters of pink, white, lilac, or purple flowers on stalks above deciduous, medium green foliage.
Height: 5 to 20 feet, depending on variety.
Growing instructions: Set 6 feet apart. To keep plant tidy, remove suckers that grow from base of plant. In damp climates, foliage often hosts mildew during the summer. This will not harm the plant but can be unsightly. If that bothers you, apply any commercially available fungus spray, such as Captan, according to manufacturer's instructions.

· · ·

Use in potpourri: Purple or lilac-colored blooms dry well, but white and pink do not. Whole flowers can be used to decorate tops of spring potpourris.
Scent: Sweet lilac.
Harvest time: At bloom time in late spring.
Recommended drying method: Hang drying.

Pussy Willow (*Salix daphnoides* or *S. acutifolia*)

· · ·

We are all familiar with the soft catkins that this plant offers.

Zones: 5 to 9.
Outdoor planting time: Spring or fall.
Light: Full sun or partial shade.
Soil: Ordinary.
Moisture: Drought resistant once established, but water regularly during prolonged summer drought.
Description: Small, fuzzy catkins appear on branches before tree leafs out.
Height: To 30 feet, depending on variety.
Growing instructions: Rapid growing, so do not plant unless you have sufficient space. Set 6 to 10 feet apart.

· · ·

Use in potpourri: Catkins dry well and add soft texture and pale gray color.
Scent: None.
Harvest time: Very early spring when in bloom.
Recommended drying method: Hang drying or water drying.

EIGHT

Making Potpourri

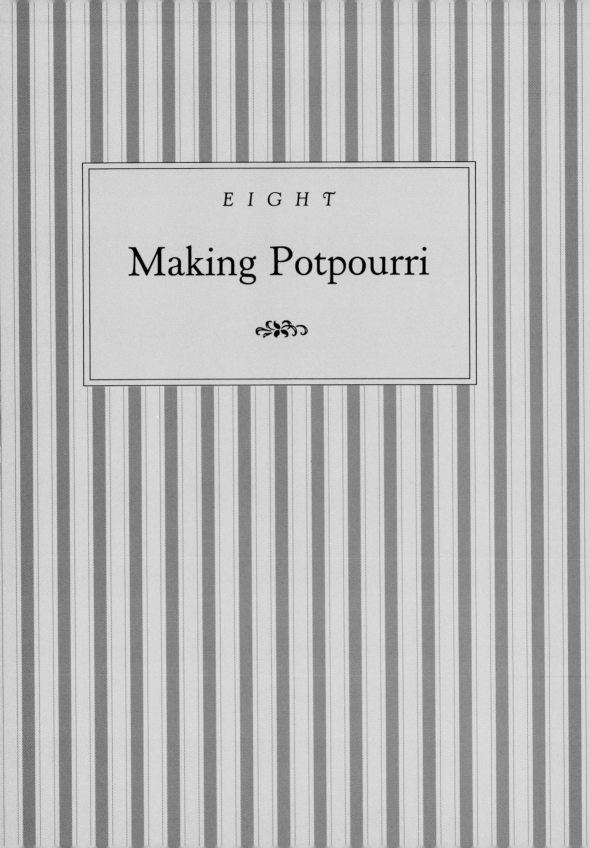

Preceding page: Hang drying is the most effective way to dry lavender.

Harvesting Potpourri Material

Now that you've installed your garden and the various herbs and flowers you've selected are growing, you will want to begin your harvest of material for your potpourri creations. Each entry in the encyclopedia sections of chapters 2 through 7 contains information about harvesting specific to that particular plant, including time of year to harvest. Here is some more general information that will be helpful.

When you pick herbs or flowers for hang drying (see below), if possible, *pick with long stems*. It is always best to pick flowers and leaves on a clear, dry day. And most plants should be harvested just after the morning dew has evaporated from the flower and leaf surfaces, but before the strong rays of the sun dilute the essential oils that give herbs and flowers their characteristic scents. In most parts of the country, during the summer, this is around 9 A.M.

Generally speaking, flower-bearing herbs are at their strongest and most fragrant just before their flowers open. Non-flower-bearing herbs are at their strongest at different times during the season; consult chapter 2 for specific in-formation. Annual and perennial flowers, shrub blossoms, and roses should be picked for drying shortly after the buds open, before the petals become damaged by wind or sun. If petals have started to fade or turn brown, don't bother to harvest them, as they will be ugly when dried. If, for some reason, you delay harvesting any particular flower and some petals have started to fade or turn brown, simply remove the unattractive petals before drying.

Any flowers that have been sprayed with chemicals are inappropriate for potpourri, as the chemicals can affect the scent as well as the color when dried. If your flower or herb material is purchased or if a friend provides you with some, be sure to check to see if it has been sprayed.

How to Dry Potpourri Material

There are a number of traditional ways to dry herbs and flowers for potpourri; some are centuries old, others more recent, and the latest, inspired by space-age technology, spanking new. However, some are more effective than others. I have tried them all and have come up with

Hang drying flowers in a shady window adds a country touch.

my own conclusions. Let's start with the traditional ways of drying material.

Hang Drying

Certainly the oldest method known, hang drying remains the most effective. Here's how you do it.

1. Collect herbs or flowers. *Be sure you pick them with long stems.*

2. *Strip all leaves from stems of flowers* before hanging them up to dry.

3. Put six stems or stalks to a bunch. Tie the bunch together with twine or wrap a rubber band around it 1 inch from the end. (Rubber bands are more effective; as the stems shrink, the rubber bands continue to hold them tight.)

4. Label each bunch. When dried, many herbs look very much alike—don't trust your memory.

5. Hang the bunches *upside down* in a dry, warm, dark place for from two days to two weeks, depending on the particular herb or flower you are drying, since some dry more quickly than others.

If you don't have a dark location to use for

hang drying, select a place that is out of strong sun. Light tends to fade colors in drying material. If you do not have the option of a dim or dark place or a place out of strong sunlight, cover each bunch of material with a paper bag, tie the open top of the bag around the stems with string, then hang—bag and all.

There are many places in the home that are suitable for hang drying potpourri material. Closets, attics, dry cellars are all fine as long as they are dry, warm, and don't receive strong sunlight. However, I found that drying in an outdoor shed or garage was *not* suitable, for damp nighttime air caused mildew and mold to form on the material.

You might want to think in terms of using the drying material as part of your interior decor. What could be more attractive than bundles of drying herbs and flowers hanging from ceilings in the kitchen or dining room, or even the living room, for that matter? If you use the kitchen for drying, avoid placing material near the stove or sink, as steam and spray can impede drying. Bathrooms are not suitable for drying for the same reasons.

There are many ways to hang potpourri material. You can drive nails or pegs into walls, ceilings, beams, or planks and hang individual varieties of herbs and flowers on them. You can use antique or reproduction herb drying racks, old laundry racks, swivel towel racks, or blanket stands, hung on walls or freestanding, and tie bundles on them. Or make your own rack; it's a matter of simple carpentry, of nailing lath on a frame, copying a photograph of a rack that appeals to you. Perhaps the easiest method is to tie the herb bunches to a clothes hanger hung on a rod or hook. Just about anything that will support a hanging bunch of drying material is suitable. *But be*

sure when you hang the material that the bunches are far enough apart so that they don't tangle or crush each other and so that air circulates around and between them. This will hasten the drying process.

When *bone* dry—and all material to be stored *must* be bone dry or it will turn into an ugly, mildewed, rotten mess—remove the herbs and flowers from the hanging area. Thresh the leaves from herbs and remove dried flowers from their stalks. Store different varieties of herbs and flowers separately in airtight containers (I find old 1-quart mayonnaise or canning jars perfect for this purpose), carefully label each, and store until ready to use in potpourri creations. Keep in mind that the jars of dried material are very handsome, and can be used on a shelf in the kitchen or dining room as interior decor. Canning jars have zinc lids that are attractive and the lids of mayonnaise

A simple rack (like those used for drying clothes) is a great help in hang drying material, in this case artemisia.

When hang drying potpourri material, use it as a temporary decorative accent in your house.

jars can be spray painted to make them more appealing.

The hang-drying process is as easy as that. *But not quite!* There were a few things I discovered in the course of drying that were not mentioned in any of the books I had read about potpourri.

KEEPING DRIED MATERIAL DRY

In most parts of the country, spring and fall are very pleasant seasons of the year, mild and not particularly wet. However, along with summer comes heat and humidity! On the east end of Long Island, where I live, summers are very humid, and I found that during the dog days of July and August, material that I had hung up to dry started to sport mold and mildew. I solved the problem by starting the drying process for a few days by hanging and then, if it was unduly damp, finishing it off by oven-drying. This process is outlined on page 108.

Still not satisfied that material was thoroughly dry, and to prevent any mold from making its way into my closed jars, I add about two tablespoons of uncooked rice to every container of drying material. The rice absorbs any moisture left in the material or in the container. Remove the rice later, by sifting through a colander.

Even though I was positive the flowers and leaves were bone-dry, I began to notice deterioration of some of the collected material inside some of the jars. Upon close examination, I discovered this was caused by small moths. Tiny, hitherto unseen, eggs, which were on the flowers or herb leaves when harvested, were apparently hatching into tiny larva, nibbling away at the plant material and turning into pesky small moths. So I place five or six

moth balls in each jar and cover them tightly. Of course, the material smells of camphor; however, before I'm ready to start creating potpourris, I remove the moth balls and the lids of the containers and air the material. After one week, all trace of camphor smell vanishes.

Air Drying

Air drying is another traditional method. To do this you need flat surfaces through which air can circulate. Some options are old window screens set on a supporting platform (you can use bricks or boxes as support), flat baskets, or cotton muslin attached to lath frames or hung up like a hammock. If space is at a premium, as long as air is permitted to circulate between them, you can devise a system of

Here rose petals air dry on gauze that has been stapled to a large picture frame.

stacking drying trays one on top of another. Drying trays are sold at many herb or health food shops, at some garden centers or nurseries, and through mail-order sources (see Sources for Potpourri Material).

This system is used for drying quantities of loose petals, individual leaves, or small flower heads, so when you harvest it is not necessary to pick flowers with long stems. Delphiniums, marigolds, peonies, roses, larkspur, lilies, zinnias, carnations, tulips, daffodils, crocuses, *Iris reticulata* and *I. danfordiae,* and bachelor's buttons can all be air dried.

Feathery flowers such as astilbe, celosia, and wild Queen Anne's Lace dry better when hung. Although hang drying is a better method for drying bunches of herb material, if for some reason you prefer to dry the leaves individually, they can be air dried on screens as well. Here's how you do it.

1. Follow the same recommendations as in hang drying in regard to selecting a drying area.

2. Cut the drying material from the garden.

3. If you wish to dry petals separately, remove them from the flower heads and spread on the air drying surface in a single layer. If you wish to dry complete flower heads, place them in a single layer in rows, with their heads facing up. If you wish to dry leaves with stems or single-stem flowers, lay them down in a random manner, but don't let them overlap.

4. Each day, move petals around or turn the flower heads. The material should be dry in two to ten days, depending on the humidity and the moisture in the leaves and flowers.

If humid conditions slow down the drying process, and mildew and mold become evi-dent, finish drying in an oven. This process is outlined on page 108.

When *bone-dry,* thresh the leaves from the herb stalks or collect the dried petals or whole flowers, storing different varieties of herbs and flowers separately in airtight containers, following my instructions in "Hang Drying" and my recommendations for beating moisture and mildew.

Water Drying

This is another of the old-fashioned, traditional ways to dry material. I tried it and found it took about a week longer to dry than hang drying or air drying. However, it is an easy method requiring no preparation and is effective for drying gift bouquets.

1. Place the harvested cutting material or gift bouquet upright in a container filled about ¼ full with water.

2. Place the container in a warm area out of the sun.

3. The water will slowly evaporate, and flowers will dry slowly and naturally. To be sure the material is bone-dry, you can finish off the drying in the oven (see page 108).

Store different varieties of herbs and flowers separately in airtight containers, following my instructions in "Hang Drying" and my special recommendations for beating moisture and mildew on page 105.

Opposite: To water dry plants, in this case forsythia branches and magnolia blossoms, just place the container and the cut material in an out-of-the-way place and let the water evaporate.

Oven Drying

In the event you do not have the space to hang or air dry material or should you need material in short order, you can dry in the oven. And, beyond that, to assure bone-dry material and avoid mildew and mold forming when the material is stored, it is a good idea to subject all hang dried or air dried material to oven drying. Here's how you do it.

1. Set the oven at 100° F and leave the door slightly ajar, so that any lingering moisture can escape.
2. Set the drying material on cookie sheets, one layer deep, and place in the oven.
3. Watch carefully, turning the material every fifteen minutes. Drying should take from fifteen minutes to several hours. When material is crisp and brittle, remove it from oven. Store it as for hang dried material.

Microwave Drying

Drying flowers and leaves in a microwave oven is the latest method of preparing material for potpourri, and it is one of the quickest and most effective, for flowers retain their brilliant color and herb leaves their rich greens when dried. Keep in mind that you must not leave the microwave oven unattended while drying material. Here's how you do it.

1. Place whole flower heads, petals, or herb leaves on a paper towel and set on the floor of the microwave oven.
2. Dry at full power for one minute. Flowers may spin around in place within the oven.
3. If not totally dry after one minute, dry for another thirty seconds at full power. Check again for dryness. Continue drying in thirty-second increments at full power, until material is bone-dry.
4. Store as for hang dried material.

I found that microwaving material kills all potential insects, so adding moth balls to containers is unnecessary.

Drying in Silica Gel

Silica gel is indispensable when you wish to dry larger, whole flowers. There are old-fashioned, traditional ways of doing this, using salt and/or sand; however, they can be messy, often take from six to eight weeks for drying, and the results are never assured. However, if you use silica gel—available in craft shops, florist supply stores, some florist shops, or through mail-order houses (see Sources for Potpourri Material)—and follow instructions carefully, success is almost always achieved.

Drying individual blossoms or petals in silica gel is an easy way to provide colorful finishes for a potpourri.

Whole roses, mini-rosebuds, delphiniums, camellias, lilies, daffodils, calendulas, and other large blossoms can be successfully dried in silica gel. One advantage to this drying method is that blossoms retain considerable color intensity. And, even when you might opt for a potpourri in subdued colors, a few bright blossoms, scattered throughout or used to decorate the surface, add a lovely, distinctive touch to your creations. Also, more fragile blossoms, such as cosmos, which do not dry well when hung, air dried, or oven dried, do not shrink to nothing when dried in silica gel.

If you purchase a silica gel flower drying kit, complete instructions for drying blossoms are usually included. If you purchase a quantity of silica gel, here's how you use it.

1. Select blossoms that are at the peak of their bloom, as these retain their color and hold together better when dried.

2. Fill any airtight, flat container, such as a metal cookie or plastic refrigerator container, with about 1 inch of silica gel. If the container is not airtight, you can seal it with freezer or masking tape.

3. Remove most of the stem and place the blossoms face up in the powdery silica gel. If you are drying flat-petaled blossoms, like daisies and gerbera, or single leaves of herbs, place them face down in the powder. Press the blossoms gently into the silica gel, making sure that the inside of the blossoms are also covered.

4. Sprinkle silica gel over the entire blossom or leaf and between the flower petals until it is completely covered. As you do this be careful not to disturb the natural arrangement of the petals.

5. Seal the container. The blossoms should be dry in two to seven days.

The most important aspect of drying flowers successfully in silica gel is to be sure the flowers are dry but not too dry, that is, not so brittle they shatter when you remove them from the powder. You will have to experiment with each flower you dry in order to ascertain the correct drying times. Check the flowers every day until they've reached the point where they're dry but not excruciatingly fragile. It takes roughly two to three days for thin-petaled flowers to dry, five to seven days for fleshier flower heads.

When flowers or leaves are ready, gently remove them from the powder with a slotted spoon. If any powder remains clinging to petals or leaves, gently brush it off with a soft, watercolor paintbrush.

Store the flowers and leaves in airtight containers until ready to use. Place a small quantity of silica gel in the bottom of the containers to absorb any moisture that might remain, and to guard against any dampness. As with the microwave method, there is no insect infestation in silica dried material, so adding moth balls to storage jars is unnecessary.

MAKING POTPOURRI

Now that you've harvested and dried the blossoms and herbs, it is time to begin creating your collection of fragrant potpourris. First, some basic information on what supplies you will need. The basic ingredients of all potpourris are: dried plant materials, essential oils, a fixative, and spices.

Dried Plant Material

Dried foliage, herbs, flower material, and fruit are used for their scent and/or for their color. Foliage, herbs, and flowers you can grow in your own potpourri garden have been covered in chapters 2 through 7. There is also much dried material, of plants often impossible to grow at home or in our climate, available through mail-order houses (see Sources for Potpourri Material).

I have found that my home-dried herbs and blossoms are much more intense in color and scent than any I have purchased from mail-order houses. But, in the event your crop fails or you don't get around to planting one particular herb or flower you wish to use, or if you want to include some exotic material in your potpourris, you can always order by mail. Beyond the plants included in previous chapters, here is a sample of some of the more exotic material available.

Cedarwood chips	Pinecones
Eucalyptus leaves	Rose hips
Frankincense (whole)	Sandalwood chips
Hawthorn berries	Senna pods
Hibiscus flowers	Tilia flowers
Myrrh (cut)	Tonka beans
Patchouli leaves	*Uva-ursi* leaves

Much of the plant material described in the previous chapters is also available. Those most likely of use to you are:

Chamomile	Lemon verbena
Lavender	Rosebuds

Beyond gathering all kinds of wild *seed pods, evergreen cones,* and *berries* in the wild, you will also want to include dried *citrus peel* and *apples* in your potpourri closet. Lemons, oranges, tangerines, and limes all dry well and retain their brilliant color. You can dry this material at any time during the year. Whenever you use a fresh lemon, lime, or orange, save the rinds. To dry, peel the rind from the fruit, cut it into small strips, place in a bowl or basket, and let dry naturally. Every few days mix the rind around a bit. In about two weeks it should be ready for use.

Apples are a fragrant and attractive addition to any potpourri, particularly those you plan for the fall. To dry them, slice the apples as thin as possible, coat with lemon juice to prevent browning, and dry on a screen in the sun or in a 100° F oven until dry (from one to two hours). You can also dry apple squares if you prefer that shape to slices. To do this cut ½-inch cubes and dry as above. It will take considerably longer to dry cubes than slices.

Essential Oils

Oils are used to enhance and fortify the scents of the natural materials and must be purchased. They are packaged in small bottles ranging in size from ⅛ ounce to 1 ounce, and can be expensive (anywhere from $2 up to $50, depending on the quality and scent), but since you use a very small amount in making each batch of potpourri, they go a long way. Essential oils are available in many retail outlets: craft shops, health food stores, herb shops, potpourri specialty shops, and occasionally at florists. However, selection often is limited. Usually you can find lavender, rose, honeysuckle, sandalwood, pine or balsam, and per-

Dried whole camellia flowers add striking decorative accents.

❧❦❧

haps gardenia. Beyond that, some shops can
order other oils from wholesale houses for you.
However, a much larger selection is available
from mail-order supply houses (see Sources for
Potpourri Material). Do not, incidentally, try

to use your favorite perfume or eau de cologne.
There is not enough concentrated oil in them
to effectively scent a potpourri.

Prices vary widely, but quality varies widely
as well, and as with almost everything else,
you get what you pay for. I think you will
find, as I did, that the better, more expensive
oils are far more concentrated, offer scents that
last much longer than cheaper oils, and have
a pure, natural scent. Some of the less expensive oils smell decidedly artificial, like cheap
perfume, particularly the floral-scented offerings. In any case, if you're buying oil in a retail
outlet, let your nose be the judge. If it smells
artificial, your finished potpourri will as well;
don't buy it.

My experience has been that despite differ-
ing prices, most of the mail-order offerings have
been satisfactory. However (and the price is
higher than other houses), Caswell & Massey
Co. Ltd. stocks the greatest variety of oils and
they are unquestionably the best available.

Of course, if you have an unlimited budget
for your project, cost will be of no concern to
you, but like most of us, you might have to
pick and choose your scents to fit your budget.
If it is possible to offer a list of oils that are
utterly indispensable to the potpourri gardener, these six, which will help you get started
and which offer the greatest versatility when
combined with naturally dried material, herbs,
and spices, are it.

- A woodsy scent such as bayberry, pine, or
  balsam
- A citrus scent such as lemon, orange, or tangerine
- A light floral scent such as honeysuckle, sweet
  pea, violet, mimosa, or lily-of-the-valley
- Nostalgic lavender

- An old-fashioned favorite, lemon verbena
- Perhaps the most popular of all, rose

Just for the purpose of offering you alternatives and to acquaint you with the vast list of possibilities, here are some other oils that are currently available.

Allspice	Lime
Anise	Lotus
Apple blossom	Mace
Apricot kernel	Magnolia
Banana	Mandarin
Bergamot	Mignonette
Birch	Myrrh
Bitter almond	Narcissus
Blueberry	Nutmeg
Carnation	Oak moss
Cedarwood	Oleander
Cinnamon	Orange blossom
Clove	Patchouli
Coconut	Peach
Coriander	Rose geranium
Cranberry	Rosemary
Eucalyptus	Sandalwood
Fougere (floral scent)	Sassafras
Frangipani	Stock
Frankincense	Strawberry
Freesia	Styrax
Gardenia	Tea rose
Grapefruit	Thyme
Heliotrope	Tuberose
Hemlock	Vanilla
Hyacinth	Verbena
Jasmine	Vetiver
Lemon grass	Wisteria
Lilac	Ylang-ylang

And, lo and behold, one house even offers skunk oil!

Fixative

This is another ingredient essential in making potpourri. Fixatives absorb the essential oils you add to the dried material, helping to maintain the scent over a long period of time. Without fixative, oils simply evaporate, along with any scent in the potpourri. Most fixatives impart a delicate, exotic fragrance to the creation and there are many different kinds that are satisfactory for potpourri use. But with one exception, you must purchase these also. Some craft shops, health food stores, and herb shops offer potpourri fixatives. But, to save time in locating one that does, it is perhaps best to write to the mail-order houses (see Sources for Potpourri Material) and order direct from them. Here are your choices:

- *Orris root* (mild, violet scent). This is far and away the most readily available fixative in local shops, the least expensive, and the most effective fixative ingredient known. I have experimented with others and found them to be either difficult to work with, difficult to locate, or inferior in staying power. Orris root is made from the rhizomes (roots) of certain varieties of iris. Once dug and cleaned, they are dried until hard as rock. Then the rhizomes are either ground into powder or chopped into pieces. In most potpourris, *use only chopped orris,* since powdered orris clings to dried material and gives it a dusty, mildewed look. Avoid using the powdered form in sachets or pillows, as the powder can sift through the cloth, leaving a residue on clothes or linens in drawers and on bedding. If you plan on keeping your potpourri in covered opaque jars, powdered orris will be fine.
- *Balsam tolu or balsam peru* (light scent).

These are available either as oil or resin. Both are sticky and somewhat difficult to work with, though they impart a very special scent to light floral potpourris. For the more advanced potpourri artisan.

• *Benzoin gum* (strong, balsam scent). Another gummy substance that has a very powerful smell and is difficult to work with, but it enhances heavy floral scented creations.

• *Calamus root* (mild, violet scent). Similar to orris root, but far less readily available.

• *Frankincense gum or oil* (spicy, balsamic odor). Adds an exotic scent to potpourris. It is particularly effective in holiday potpourris.

• *Myrrh gum or oil* (spicy, woodsy scent). Less powerful than frankincense. Another effective fixative for holiday potpourris.

• *Oakmoss* (light scent, but used mainly for silver color). A lichen that grows in southern Europe, not always readily available, but effective with floral potpourris.

• *Patchouli* (strong woodsy scent). From the Far East and the Philippines, it is used primarily for its dark green color. As a fixative, it is long lasting and combines well with spicy potpourris.

• *Sandalwood* (sweet, exotic scent). From Asia, imparts little of its own scent, but retains essential oils especially well. Effective with exotic potpourris.

• *Vetiver* (lovely earthy scent). Vetiver is fine textured and pale yellow in color. It blends nicely with rose.

There are two fixatives that you occasionally may see: ambergris and musk oil. Ambergris oil is made from a substance found in the intestines of sperm whales and musk from the glands of the Asian male musk deer. Both are endangered species. These materials should not be offered for sale.

The only effective fixative that you can make at home is one made of lemon or orange rinds. If, for one reason or other, you cannot find or buy orris root, you can dry the rinds and use them instead. But all potpourris you make will then have a considerable lemon or orange citrus scent.

Spices

There are many spices that you can buy in your local supermarket that are delightful additions to potpourri creations. Among them are:

Allspice (whole and ground)
Anise seed, star anise
Bay leaf (whole)
Cinnamon (sticks and ground)
Clove (whole and ground)
Coriander seeds
Ginger root (pieces or slices)
Juniper berries
Lemon rind
Mace (ground)
Nutmeg (whole and ground)
Orange rind

THE TOOLS OF THE CRAFT

In addition to the ingredients for making potpourri, you will need the tools of the craft. To make things easier for you, all quantities of ingredients for potpourris included in the recipe section (chapter 9) are given in quarts, pints, teaspoons, and tablespoons, as in food recipes. So you probably already have most of

Spices, like the nutmeg and cinnamon pictured here with other potpourri ingredients, can add pizzazz to your creations, and are usually already in your kitchen.

the tools right in your kitchen. Here is what you need:

- Measuring cups, plastic preferred (¼, ⅓, ½, and 1 cup)
- Measuring spoons, plastic preferred (⅛, ¼, ½, 1 teaspoon, 1 tablespoon)
- Quart jars with lids for storing potpourri while it ripens. These can be 1-quart canning jars or empty mayonnaise jars, or for larger quantities, 2-quart or 1-gallon jars. (Empty 1-gallon mayonnaise jars are usually available in the deli department in your local supermarket. They are usually just thrown out.)
- Wooden spoons or chopsticks for mixing. Do not use metal spoons as they affect the scent of the potpourri.

- Small eye droppers. If you don't have these around the house, you can buy them at your local drugstore. They are very inexpensive.
- Large pottery or china bowls for mixing. Do not use metal bowls as the metal affects the scent of the potpourri.
- A pair of scissors for cutting material too large for the potpourri you are creating.

Since you have worked hard growing all of the material you need and scouted around for oils, fixatives, and spices, now is the time for the rewards of your labor, the utter enjoyment of creating potpourris. I fashion mine on a large kitchen table adjacent to a sunny window overlooking the garden, assembling all ingredients and then putting them together. When I do this, I always feel I'm a bit of a wizard, measuring ingredients, adding oils and fixatives, smelling to see if I should add this or that. It is an immensely rewarding and gratifying endeavor. And then, when I'm through, and all of the potpourris are bottled and displayed while they age, I look forward to placing them here and there throughout the house and giving them as gifts to friends. I have yet to find one recipient who wasn't utterly enchanted with a container of potpourri.

SACHETS

Beyond making potpourri for use in bowls and containers, you might want to make some sachets to use in scenting drawers and closets. Here's an easy way to do it.

1. Using pinking shears, cut a square of fabric 6½ by 7½ inches.
2. Fold it in half so that the wrong side of

the fabric is on the outside and the sachet measures 3¼ inches across by 7½ inches high.

3. Stitch two sides of the fabric together, leaving the top, narrow side open.

4. Turn inside out so that the right side of the fabric is on the outside; press with an iron.

5. Fold 1½ inches of the top inside the sachet and press again.

6. Fill with potpourri and tie with a ribbon that complements the fabric color.

A Few Last Words Before You Start

The recipes for making potpourris are included in the next chapter. But before you start in, here are a few things to keep in mind.

• Try to keep dried leaves and flowers as whole as possible, rather than crumbling them up into small pieces. In other words, when you stir your potpourri, *stir gently*. Part of the enchantment of potpourri is to be able to identify the dried material in the creation. You may have found when you have purchased commercially available potpourri that although the scent is there, much of the dried material is unidentifiable, and usually brownish in color. This is because many of these contain a large percentage of what is called "filler." I inquired at one outlet about filler in the potpourri and the owner told me, without hesitation, that she puts dried autumn leaves in the blender, cuts them up and adds them to potpourri. I asked what percentage of the ingredients were dried leaves and she replied, "About three-fourths of it." "My goodness," I thought. "Ten dollars for two cups of dried autumn leaves is no bargain." This is the ad-

Place potpourri in cloth bags to create lovely scented sachets for closets and drawers.

vantage of growing your own material and making your own potpourri. You don't have to worry about stretching expensive dried material, for you can grow all you need.

• If you use the best oils and are not stingy with the amount you use, your potpourri will retain its scent far longer than any you purchase in retail outlets. And then, if the scent becomes faint, you have the oil on hand to renew the glorious aroma.

NINE

The Recipes

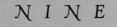

Spring · Summer
Autumn · Holiday

Preceding page: Here Victorian Lavender Pot-pourri (recipe on page 129) adds a charming touch to a nightstand in a guest room.

And now, the recipes. This is what you've been waiting for. You've planted, harvested, and dried all the materials and purchased whatever fixatives, oils, and exotic dried material you wish to include in your creations.

Please note that in almost all of the recipes, I have included only one essential oil. This is because a pure, uncomplicated scent appeals more to me than a busy one that makes it difficult to identify particular aromas. However, there is no reason why you can't experiment with small portions of a potpourri and combine scents to see if the combination is pleasing to you. If you feel your potpourri needs sweetening, try a touch of cinnamon or jasmine oil. If the scent is rather bland, add lemon or lemon verbena oil. To add depth, add a touch of sandalwood and to tone down a scent that is too strong add more dried material.

I have divided the recipes into those that I feel are appropriate for each season: spring, summer, autumn, and the winter holidays. But if a recipe offered for spring appeals to you in the fall, or vice versa, by all means create it and enjoy it.

SPRING

With the passing of winter, the miniature, spring bulbs begin to bloom. Many are suitable for drying and add sparkling color and enchantment to spring potpourri creations. And then, as the season progresses, the parade of spring blooming flowers and shrubs continues: pussy willow, forsythia, daffodils, hyacinths, tulips, azalea and rhododendron, and scores of other flowering plants. Experiment with drying any that you might have on your property, as the recipes offered on the following pages are mere guidelines in terms of dried ingredients.

The recipes in this section include the lighter, sweet-smelling scents of spring: sweet pea, freesia, hyacinth, daffodil, violet, lily-of-the-valley, honeysuckle, magnolia, orange blossom, and the noncitrus fruity scents: peach and strawberry. If any one of these scents is among your favorites, you can substitute these oils for those recommended.

Scarlett's Revenge

. . .

Magnolia is the scent of spring in the South, land of Scarlett O'Hara, after whom this creation is named. As you breathe the scent, visions of Southern belles and Atlanta in flames will come to mind. This creation, filled with spring blossoms, probably is most suitable for the bedroom; however, as with all potpourris, you can place it wherever you wish. Substitute orange blossom oil for magnolia, if you like; if you do, change the name of the potpourri to Southern Comfort.

3 tablespoons chopped orris root
½ teaspoon magnolia oil
1 cup dried pink camellia flowers

Camellias and candlelight set off Scarlett's Revenge, a magnolia-scented potpourri. That's not Atlanta in flames in the background, but a gently flickering fire.

1 cup dried pastel-colored azalea or
  rhododendron flowers
¾ cup dried lemon balm leaves
¼ cup dried pink hyacinth flowers
½ cup dried chamomile flowers

1. Place the orris root in a quart-sized glass or porcelain jar with the magnolia oil and mix thoroughly with a wooden spoon or chopstick. Cover the container with a lid and put aside for three days to allow oil to absorb into fixative. Shake every day.

2. After three days, pour the fixative-oil combination into a large glass or porcelain bowl. (Do not use a metal bowl, as the scent will be affected.) Then add the remaining ingredients and mix thoroughly.

3. Add additional camellia or azalea flowers or lemon balm leaves (about ½ cup) to make 1 quart of potpourri. Mix thoroughly again.

4. Place the potpourri in the jar and cover again. After two weeks the potpourri should have a strong magnolia scent. If it does not, add another ½ teaspoon magnolia oil. In either case, let sit another two weeks in a dark place. Every few days either shake the jar or mix the potpourri with a wooden spoon or chopstick.

If you like, at this point you can try adding a touch of lemon oil to a small portion of the potpourri to see if you like the combined scent. If you do, place the potpourri back in the jar, add ½ teaspoon lemon oil, close the jar, and let sit for another two weeks.

5. Place the finished potpourri in a favorite container and decorate the surface with some dried whole camellia flowers and display.

Peaches and Cream

. . .

Oils of late spring fruit added to dried material offer lovely fragrances suitable for the kitchen as well as other parts of the house. I placed a bowl of this potpourri in my china closet and after two years, each time I open it the delicate aroma of peaches still wafts through the room. To be most effective visually, the dried flower material should be pale yellow or cream, with most of the leaf material silver. To encourage the touching of the potpourri, both pussy willows and lamb's ears, which, like peach skins, are fuzzy, are included.

This fragrance is so lovely, if you don't have the dried material suggested, don't let this stop you. Combine the oil with any material available and although the visual effect may not be as pleasing, you will still be able to enjoy the aroma.

3 tablespoons chopped orris root
½ teaspoon peach oil
1 cup dried pussy willows
½ cup dried betony or lamb's ears
1 cup dried artemisia
¼ cup dried pale yellow button
  chrysanthemums
½ cup dried miniature daffodils
½ cup dried orange crocus
½ cup dried sweet woodruff

1. Place the orris root in a quart-sized glass or porcelain jar with the peach oil and mix thoroughly with a wooden spoon or chopstick. Cover the container with a lid and put aside for three days to allow the oil to absorb into the fixative. Shake every day.

2. After three days, pour the fixative-oil

Peaches and Cream Potpourri is used to enhance a collection of eggs.

combination into a large glass or porcelain bowl. (Do not use a metal bowl, as the scent will be affected.) Then add the remaining ingredients and mix thoroughly.

3. Add additional artemisia or sweet woodruff (about ¼ cup) to make 1 quart of potpourri. Mix thoroughly.

4. Place the potpourri in the jar and cover again. After two weeks the potpourri should have a strong peach scent. If it does not, add another ½ teaspoon peach oil. In either case, let sit another two weeks in a dark place. Every few days either shake the jar or mix the potpourri with a wooden spoon or chopstick.

If you like, at this point you can try adding a touch of almond oil to a small portion of the potpourri to see if you like the combined scent. If you do, place the potpourri in the jar, add ½ teaspoon almond oil, close, and let sit for another two weeks.

5. Place the finished potpourri in a favorite container, decorate the surface with some whole lamb's ears, and display.

Royal Romanov Strawberry Parfait

. . .

After the Russian revolution, one of the Romanov grand dukes fled to the South of France. Fortunately for him, he was able to leave Russia with valuables sufficient to enable him to live in high style. While staying at the Hotel du Cap in Antibes, each evening he ordered a plate of *fraise des bois,* the highly aromatic wild strawberries of France, brought up to his room. The strawberries were not meant to be eaten. He ordered the berries crushed with a fork, so he could enjoy their scent through the night. With this highly fragrant potpourri, you can enjoy the same decadent pleasure of strawberry scent.

An ideal potpourri for the kitchen, Royal Romanov Strawberry Parfait, decorates the counter of an old Hoosier chest.

3 tablespoons chopped orris root
½ teaspoon strawberry oil
1½ cups dried pineapple mint
1 cup dried candytuft
¼ cup dried thrift or any other blossom that dries to a pink color
¼ cup dried whole red tulip petals
½ cup dried whole betony or lamb's ears

1. Place the orris root in a quart-sized glass or porcelain jar with the strawberry oil and mix thoroughly with a wooden spoon or chopstick. Cover the container with a lid and put aside for three days to allow the oil to absorb into the fixative. Shake every day.

2. After three days, pour the fixative-oil combination into a large glass or porcelain bowl. (Do not use a metal bowl, as the scent will be affected.) Then add the pineapple mint, candytuft, and thrift, and mix thoroughly.

3. Add additional pineapple mint (about ¼ cup) to make 1 quart of potpourri. Mix thoroughly.

4. Place the potpourri in the jar and cover. After two weeks the potpourri should have a strong strawberry scent. If it does not, add another ½ teaspoon strawberry oil. In either case, let sit another two weeks in a dark place. Every few days either shake the jar or mix the potpourri with a wooden spoon or chopstick.

5. Place the finished potpourri in a favorite container, decorate surface with the red tulip petals and betony, and display.

Heavenly Honeysuckle

. . .

One of the most cherished spring scents is that of honeysuckle. Remember the days of our budding adolescence, the honeyed aroma of this wild plant wafting through the air during a balmy June night, and the tender torment of unrequited young love? One of the most readily available oils, combined with apple-scented herbs honeysuckle is utterly intoxicating. If you wish to add some rose oil to the potpourri, you can change the name to Honeysuckle Rose, place a Marlene Dietrich record on the stereo, and drift away into your own private dream world.

3 tablespoons chopped orris root
½ teaspoon honeysuckle oil
1½ cups dried apple mint
½ cup dried chamomile flowers
½ cup dried feverfew flowers
¼ cup dried daffodil flowers
¼ cup assorted dried blue spring bulb flowers
    (Iris reticulata, grape hyacinth, crocus, scilla, and/or hyacinth)

1. Place the orris root in a quart-sized glass or porcelain jar with the honeysuckle oil and mix thoroughly with a wooden spoon or chopstick. Cover the container with a lid and put aside for three days to allow the oil to absorb into the fixative. Shake every day.

2. After three days, pour the fixative-oil combination into a large glass or porcelain bowl. (Do not use a metal bowl, as the scent will be affected.) Then add the remaining ingredients and mix thoroughly.

3. Add additional apple mint (about ½ cup) to make 1 quart potpourri. Mix thoroughly again.

4. Place the potpourri in the jar and cover. After two weeks the potpourri should have a strong honeysuckle scent. If it does not, add another ½ teaspoon honeysuckle oil. In either case, let it sit another two weeks in a dark

Heavenly Honeysuckle Potpourri scents a country bedroom.

place. Every few days either shake the jar or mix the potpourri with a wooden spoon or chopstick.

If you like, at this point you can try adding a touch of rose oil to a small portion of the potpourri to see if you like the combined scent. If you do, place the potpourri back in the jar, add ½ teaspoon rose oil, close, and let sit for another two weeks.

5. Place the finished potpourri in a favorite container and display.

April in Paris

. . .

In France, on the first day of spring, the French sport a lily-of-the-valley sprig in their lapels or in their hair. Depending on your budget and your predilection, any of the lighter scented oils is appropriate for this potpourri. And if you've never been to France, these scents will make you wish you had.

3 tablespoons chopped orris root
½ teaspoon sweet pea, hyacinth, violet, or lily-of-the-valley oil
1 cup dried artemisia or santolina
¾ cup dried pussy willow
½ cup dried pansy flowers
¼ cup dried daffodil flowers
¼ cup dried assorted blue spring bulb flowers (Iris reticulata, grape hyacinth, crocus, scilla, and/or hyacinth)

1. Place the orris root in a quart-sized glass or porcelain jar with the oil of your choice and mix thoroughly with a wooden spoon or chopstick. Cover the container with a lid and put

A few faux pearls add further interest to April in Paris, a lily-of-the-valley-scented potpourri. Perfect for the boudoir!

aside for three days to allow the oil to absorb into the fixative. Shake every day.

2. After three days, pour the fixative-oil combination into a large glass or porcelain bowl. (Do not use a metal bowl, as the scent will be affected.) Then add the artemisia or santolina, pussy willow, and pansies, and mix thoroughly.

3. Add additional dried artemisia or santolina (about ¼ cup) to make 1 quart of potpourri. Mix thoroughly.

4. Place the potpourri in the jar and cover. After two weeks the potpourri should have a strong scent. If it does not, add ½ teaspoon more oil. In either case, let sit another two weeks in a dark place. Every few days either

shake the jar or mix the potpourri with a wooden spoon or chopstick.

If you like, at this point you can try adding a touch of another light scented oil to a small portion of the potpourri to see if you like the combined scent. If you do, place the potpourri back in the jar, add ½ teaspoon of the oil, close, and let sit for another two weeks.

5. Place the finished potpourri in a favorite container, decorate the top with the daffodils and assorted blue spring bulb flowers, and display.

SUMMER

The summer potpourris include two of the all-time favorites, one made with lemon verbena, the other with rose. Whereas the spring scents are either delicate and light or fruity, the summer scents offer refreshing citrus scents or the sultry, heavier aromas given off by many summer flowers.

Summer Nostalgia

· · ·

During the Roaring Twenties, heavier scented perfumes, complementing the scents of the summer garden, were very much in vogue. Here is a potpourri designed to evoke F. Scott Fitzgerald's Flaming Youth and the Jazz Age, the era of flappers, sheiks, raccoon coats, summer garden parties, Dixieland jazz, and an intensely vigorous Charleston. The potpourri has been designed in the colors red, white, and blue, so if you wish to make some for the Fourth of July, it will be appropriate.

3 tablespoons chopped orris root
½ teaspoon of one of the following oils: jasmine, gardenia, mignonette, mimosa, frangipani, tuberose, stephanotis, or heliotrope
1½ cups dried delphinium or larkspur flowers
1 cup dried artemisia or santolina
½ cup dried red rose petals
¼ cup dried bachelor's button or malva flowers
¼ cup dried white chrysanthemum flowers
5 or 6 whole dried red roses

1. Place the orris root in a quart-sized glass or porcelain jar with the selected oil and mix thoroughly with a wooden spoon or chopstick. Cover the container with a lid and put aside for three days to allow the oil to absorb into the fixative. Shake every day.

2. After three days, pour the fixative-oil combination into a large glass or porcelain bowl. (Do not use a metal bowl, as the scent will be affected.) Then add everything but the dried whole roses and mix together.

3. Add additional dried artemisia or santolina (about ½ cup) to make 1 quart of potpourri. Mix thoroughly.

4. Place the potpourri in the jar and cover. After two weeks the potpourri should have a strong scent. If it does not, add ½ teaspoon more of the selected oil. In either case, let sit another two weeks in a dark place. Every few days either shake the jar or mix the potpourri with a wooden spoon or chopstick.

If you like, at this point you can try adding a touch of lemon- or orange-scented oil to a small portion of the potpourri to see if you like the combined scent. If you do, place the potpourri back in the glass jar, add ½ teaspoon oil, close the jar, and let sit for another two weeks.

5. Place the finished potpourri in a favorite container, decorate the top with the whole dried red roses, and display.

Classic Old-Fashioned Rose Potpourri

. . .

Along with lavender and lemon verbena, potpourris made of rose petals are traditional favorites and have been for centuries. Here is a basic recipe you can experiment with by adding small portions of lavender, citrus, or spice-scented oils.

The most popular potpourri of them all is Classic Old-Fashioned Rose, always a welcome addition.

3 tablespoons chopped orris root
½ teaspoon rose oil
1 cup dried crushed rose petals
1½ cups dried whole rose petals
½ cup dried lavender leaves and/or flowers
½ cup dried rose-scented geranium leaves
½ cup dried whole miniature roses
6 whole dried roses

1. Place the orris root in a quart-sized glass or porcelain jar with the rose oil and mix thoroughly with a wooden spoon or chopstick. Cover the container with a lid and put aside for three days to allow the oil to absorb into the fixative. Shake every day.

2. After three days, pour the fixative-oil combination into a large glass or porcelain bowl. (Do not use a metal bowl, as the scent will be affected.) Then add everything but the 6 dried whole roses and mix thoroughly.

3. Add additional dried rose-scented geranium leaves (about ¼ cup) to make 1 quart of potpourri. Mix thoroughly.

4. Place the potpourri in the jar and cover. After two weeks the potpourri should have a strong scent. If it does not, add ½ teaspoon more rose oil. In either case, let sit another two weeks in a dark place. Every few days either shake the jar or mix the potpourri with a wooden spoon or chopstick.

If you like, at this point you can try adding a touch of lavender, lemon verbena, citrus, or a spice oil such as cinnamon, allspice, or nutmeg to a small portion of the potpourri to see if you like the combined scent. If you do, place the potpourri back in the glass jar, add ½ teaspoon of the selected oil, close the jar, and let sit for another two weeks.

5. Place the finished potpourri in a favorite container, decorate the top with the 6 whole dried roses, and display.

What could be more summery than a pitcher filled with ice-cold lemonade? Here lemon-colored lilies and Classic Lemon Verbena conspire to make this table setting a memorable one.

Classic Lemon Verbena

. . .

This is another classic scent, popular ever since the Spanish explorers brought this plant to Europe from South America during the fifteenth and sixteenth centuries. I feel the fragrance is so lovely that combining it with other oils is near sacrilege; hence, this pure scented potpourri.

3 tablespoons chopped orris root
½ teaspoon lemon verbena oil
1 cup crushed dried lemon verbena leaves
1 cup whole dried lemon verbena leaves
1 cup dried calendula flowers and/or dried chrysanthemum flowers
½ cup dried lemon-scented geranium leaves, dried lemon-scented thyme leaves, or dried patchouli

1. Place the orris root in a quart-sized glass or porcelain jar with the lemon verbena oil and mix thoroughly with a wooden spoon or chopstick. Cover the container with a lid and put aside for three days to allow the oil to absorb into the fixative. Shake every day.

2. After three days, pour the fixative-oil combination into a large glass or porcelain bowl. (Do not use a metal bowl, as the scent will be affected.) Then add the remaining ingredients and mix thoroughly.

3. Add additional lemon verbena leaves (about ¼ cup) to make 1 quart of potpourri. Mix thoroughly.

4. Place the potpourri in the jar and cover. After two weeks the potpourri should have a strong scent. If it does not, add ½ teaspoon more lemon verbena oil. In either case, let sit another two weeks in a dark place. Every few days either shake the jar or mix the potpourri with a wooden spoon or chopstick.

5. Place the finished potpourri in a favorite container and display.

Scintillating Citrus Potpourri

. . .

This potpourri is designed to transform any sourpuss into a glad rag doll. A single sniff and not only will your nose pucker up, but, more to the point, so will your lips! It is designed to add a waft of refreshment to a summer romance. Citrus-scented oils are available in lemon, lime, orange, mandarin, and tangerine. I have found tangerine to be the most invigorating.

3 tablespoons chopped orris root
½ teaspoon lemon, lime, orange, mandarin, or tangerine oil
1 cup dried orange rind
½ cup dried lemon rind
1 cup dried orange or yellow calendula flowers
¼ cup dried lemon thyme
1 cup dried lemon-scented geranium leaves, dried lemon balm leaves, or dried lemon verbena leaves

1. Place the orris root in a quart-sized glass or porcelain jar with the selected oil and mix thoroughly with a wooden spoon or chopstick. Cover the container with a lid and put aside for three days to allow the oil to absorb into the fixative. Shake every day.

2. After three days, pour the fixative-oil combination into a large glass or porcelain bowl. (Do not use a metal bowl, as the scent will be affected.) Then add the remaining ingredients and mix thoroughly.

3. Add additional dried lemon-scented geranium leaves, dried lemon balm leaves, or dried lemon verbena leaves (about ¼ cup) to make 1 quart of potpourri. Mix thoroughly.

4. Place the potpourri in the jar and cover. After two weeks the potpourri should have a strong scent. If it does not, add ½ teaspoon more oil. In either case, let sit another two weeks in a dark place. Every few days either shake the jar or mix the potpourri with a wooden spoon or chopstick.

If you like, at this point you can try adding touches of other citrus scented oils to the one you've selected. Add some to a portion of the potpourri to see if you like the combined scent. If you like the additive, add ½ teaspoon of that oil to the potpourri, close the jar, and let sit for another two weeks.

5. Place the finished potpourri in a favorite container and display.

AUTUMN

During the fall, there are all sorts of new materials available for potpourri use. The berry-producing shrubs now proudly display their fruit. Chrysanthemums are in bloom, and when dried, add flaming touches of orange, yellow, and rust to creations. All sorts of dried wild material is available. By just taking a stroll through the countryside, you'll find scores of plants with seed pods and dried foliage that you can gather and put to good use in potpourris. In the garden, the roses continue blooming and, perhaps the potpourri gardener's most essential material, lavender, is ready to harvest. If you've dried material during the spring and summer, you will find use for some of the colors in fall potpourris.

For spring potpourri, recipes featuring light floral scents were offered; in summer, recipes for heavier floral scents and lighter citrus and fruity scents. Now, in the fall, the exotic, erotic scents, such as sandalwood and lotus, as well as the most popular of all, lavender, and spicy creations are dominant.

Victorian Lavender Potpourri

· · ·

Lavender is synonymous with potpourri, unquestionably the most popular potpourri scent of all. This recipe for a Victorian lavender potpourri may evoke memories of childhood, or of a gentler era, long since gone. It is appropriate in the bathroom or bedrooms, in either open or closed containers. Just imagine how enchanted your house guests will be when you show them to their room and open the lid on a container of Victorian Lavender Potpourri. As the scent fills the room, they will already have memories of a very special visit.

3 tablespoons chopped orris root
½ teaspoon lavender oil
1½ cups dried lavender flowers
½ cup dried lavender leaves
½ cup dried orange rind
3 tablespoons dried orange firethorn berries
½ cup dried blue bachelor's buttons, larkspur or delphinium, or malva blossoms, or a combination of all
1 chopped vanilla bean or 4 chopped tonka beans
1 tablespoon whole allspice

1. Place the orris root in a quart-sized glass or porcelain jar with the lavender oil and mix thoroughly with a wooden spoon or chopstick. Cover the container with a lid and put aside for three days to allow the oil to absorb into the fixative. Shake every day.

2. After three days, pour the fixative-oil combination into a large glass or porcelain bowl. (Do not use a metal bowl, as the scent will be affected.) Then add the remaining ingredients and mix thoroughly.

3. Add additional dried lavender flowers or leaves (about ½ cup) to make 1 quart of potpourri. Mix thoroughly.

4. Place the potpourri in the jar and cover. After two weeks the potpourri should have a strong lavender scent. If it does not, add ½ teaspoon more lavender oil. In either case, let

sit another two weeks in a dark place. Every few days either shake the jar or mix the potpourri with a wooden spoon or chopstick.

If you like, at this point you can try adding a touch of rose oil to a small portion of the potpourri to see if you like the combined scent. If you do, add ½ teaspoon rose oil to the potpourri, close the jar, and let sit for another two weeks.

5. Place the finished potpourri in a favorite container, decorate the surface with some dried orange rind and pyracantha berries, and display.

Notice in the photograph of the lavender potpourri (page 116) that beyond the open bowl creation there is also a closed, glass apothecary jar layered with various dried material. To make this, place 1 tablespoon of orris root in a small jar with about ½ teaspoon of lavender oil. Allow three days for the oil to absorb into the fixative, shaking the contents each day. Then place the mixture in the bottom of an apothecary jar. Layer various materials as you see fit, keeping contrast of color and texture in mind. Fill the jar to the top, close with a lid, and display. When you wish the scent to permeate a room, simply remove the lid from the jar.

Tormenting Sandalwood

· · ·

Here's an exotic potpourri that, with your help of course, can add the perfect romantic touch to any room. More for the boudoir than the bedroom, it is seductive, evocative, and in the proper setting, utterly tormenting, suggestive of erotic harems and the forbidden pleasures of distant lands. Need more be said?

A collection of Indian and Nepalese curios is set amid Tormenting Sandalwood Potpourri.

3 tablespoons chopped orris root
½ teaspoon sandalwood oil
2 cups mixed dried yellow, orange, and rust chrysanthemum blossoms
1 cup dried red rose hips
½ cup sandalwood chips. You can substitute cedarwood chips or, in lieu of either, add more dried flowers, whole hazelnuts, or acorns.
½ cup eucalyptus or bay leaves

1. Place the orris root in a quart-sized glass or porcelain jar with the sandalwood oil and

mix thoroughly with a wooden spoon or chopstick. Cover the container with a lid and put aside for three days to allow the oil to absorb into the fixative. Shake every day.

2. After three days, pour the fixative-oil combination into a large glass or porcelain bowl. (Do not use a metal bowl, as the scent will be affected.) Then add the remaining ingredients and mix thoroughly.

3. Add additional chrysanthemum (about ½ cup) to make 1 quart of potpourri. Mix thoroughly.

4. Place the potpourri in the jar and cover. After two weeks the potpourri should have a strong sandalwood scent. If not, add another ½ teaspoon of oil. In either case, let sit for another two weeks in a dark place. Every few days either shake the jar or mix the potpourri with a wooden spoon or chopstick.

If you like, at this point you can try adding a touch of myrrh oil to a small portion of the potpourri to see if you like the combined scent. If you do, place the potpourri back in the glass jar, add ½ teaspoon of either oil, close the jar, and let sit for another two weeks in a dark place.

5. Place the finished potpourri in a favorite container and display.

Fine 'n' Dandy Carnation Potpourri can't help but inspire the man of the house to spruce up a bit.

Fine 'n' Dandy Carnation Potpourri

. . .

It used to be that no boulevardier, dandy, or fop would be seen dead on the street without a carnation boutonierre in his lapel. Sadly, those days are gone; however, this potpourri makes an inspiring gift to that man in your life whose former sartorial splendor has gotten just a bit dog-earred and shopworn.

Although carnations are available at florists all through the year and grow in the garden through summer and fall, the subtle spicy-sweet clove scent seems to be perfect for fall. The carnation petals and whole flowers you add to this creation can either be grown in the garden or salvaged from gift bouquets of carnations or, should you happen to know one, the buttonhole of a lady-killer.

3 tablespoons chopped orris root
½ teaspoon carnation oil
2 cups dried artemisia leaves and flowers
1½ cups of the following dried material, in
*   any combination: red rose petals; red*
*   carnation petals; red pineapple sage*
*   flowers and green pineapple sage leaves*
2 tablespoons whole cloves

2 tablespoons crushed cinnamon sticks
Several dried whole carnations

1. Place the orris root in a quart-sized glass or porcelain jar with the carnation oil and mix thoroughly with a wooden spoon or chopstick. Cover the container with a lid and put aside for three days to allow the oil to absorb into the fixative. Shake every day.

2. After three days, pour the fixative-oil combination into a large glass or porcelain bowl. (Do not use a metal bowl, as the scent will be affected.) Then add the remaining ingredients and mix thoroughly.

3. Add additional dried red flower petals (about ½ cup) to make 1 quart of potpourri. Mix thoroughly.

4. Place the potpourri in the jar and cover. Let sit for one month in a dark place. Every few days either shake the jar or mix the potpourri with a wooden spoon or chopstick. After two weeks the potpourri should have a strong carnation scent. If not, add another ½ teaspoon carnation oil. In either case, let sit for two more weeks. Every few days either shake the jar or mix the potpourri.

Although clove oil, similar to carnation oil in scent, is more readily available, it is far too strong for a subtle potpourri. And carnation oil has a unique sweet aroma that clove oil does not possess. If you like, at this point you can try adding a touch of lemon or lemon verbena oil to a small portion of the potpourri to see if you like the combined scent. If you do, place the potpourri back in the jar, add ½ teaspoon of either oil, close the jar, and let sit for another two weeks in a dark place.

5. Place the finished potpourri in a favorite container, decorate the surface with the dried whole carnations, and display.

Autumn Spice

. . .

The crisp, clear, chilly days of fall are always welcome after a long, hot summer. And along with them comes a hearty appetite. This is the season to enjoy old favorites: pumpkin pie, gingerbread, spice cake, and other traditional desserts, all seasoned with the robust flavors of nutmeg, allspice, and cinnamon. Here's a potpourri custom-made to accompany the flavors of fall.

Autumn Spice Potpourri scents any room with the familiar aromas of fall.

3 tablespoons chopped orris root
½ teaspoon allspice oil
½ cup dried orange calendula blossoms
½ cup dried red rose petals
½ cup dried southernwood leaves
12 whole nutmegs
3 tablespoons chopped cinnamon bark (to
  chop cinnamon bark, wrap cinnamon sticks
  in a cloth towel and bang with a hammer
  until broken into small pieces)
3 tablespoons whole allspice
1 teaspoon ground allspice
1 teaspoon ground nutmeg

1. Place the orris root in a quart-sized glass or porcelain jar with the allspice oil and mix thoroughly with a wooden spoon or chopstick. Cover the container with a lid and put aside for three days to allow the oil to absorb into the fixative. Shake every day.

2. After three days, pour the fixative-oil combination into a large glass or porcelain bowl. (Do not use a metal bowl, as the scent will be affected.) Then add the remaining ingredients and mix thoroughly.

3. Add additional dried orange calendula blossoms (about ¼ cup) to make 1 quart of potpourri. Mix thoroughly.

4. Place the potpourri in the jar and cover. After two weeks the potpourri should have a strong, spicy scent. If not, add another ½ teaspoon of oil. In either case, let sit for another two weeks in a dark place. Every few days either shake the jar or mix the potpourri with a wooden spoon or chopstick.

If you like, at this point you can try adding a touch of nutmeg oil to a small portion of the potpourri to see if you like the combined scent. If so, place the potpourri back in the jar, add ½ teaspoon of nutmeg oil, close the jar, and let sit for another two weeks in a dark place.

5. Place the finished potpourri in a favorite container, decorate the surface with more whole nutmeg, allspice, and chopped cinnamon bark, and display.

Ming Chee's Lotsa Lotus Potpourri

. . .

Another exotic scent perfect for a fall potpourri is lotus. This silver and pale yellow-colored recipe calls for using dried chamomile blossoms, which add autumn's apple scent to the potpourri.

My dear Chinese friend, Ming Chee, parted with the ancient family recipe so I might share it with you. In China it is used by young maidens to encourage would-be suitors.

Almost everyone has something Chinese in the house, be it a fan, ginger jar, figurine, or bowl. Why not fill yours up with a lotus potpourri and create a focal point somewhere in your living room? Or add a touch of class to the bedroom or guest room by placing a lotus potpourri next to the bed.

3 tablespoons chopped orris root
½ teaspoon lotus oil
1 cup dried yellow and white chrysanthemum
  petals
½ cup dried chamomile blossoms
½ cup dried sweet marjoram leaves
½ cup dried betony
½ cup dried whole yellow button
  chrysanthemums

1. Place the orris root in a quart-sized glass or porcelain jar with the lotus oil and mix

Ming Chee's Lotsa Lotus Potpourri imparts a distinctive Oriental fragrance.

thoroughly with a wooden spoon or chopstick. Cover the container with a lid and put aside for three days to allow the oil to absorb into the fixative. Shake every day.

2. After three days, pour the fixative-oil combination into a large glass or porcelain bowl. (Do not use a metal bowl, as the scent will be affected.) Then add the remaining ingredients and mix thoroughly.

3. Add additional dried yellow and white chrysanthemum petals (about ¼ cup) to make 1 quart of potpourri. Mix thoroughly.

4. Place the potpourri in the jar and cover. After two weeks the potpourri should have a strong lotus scent. If not, add another ½ teaspoon of oil. In either case, let sit for another two weeks in a dark place. Every few days either shake the jar or mix the potpourri with

a wooden spoon or chopstick.

If you like, at this point you can try adding a touch of lemon, orange, tangerine, or lime oil to see if you like the combined scent. If you do, place the potpourri back in the jar, add ½ teaspoon of the oil, close the jar, and let sit for another two weeks in a dark place.

5. Place the finished potpourri in a favorite container, decorate the surface with more dried whole yellow button chrysanthemums, and display.

HOLIDAY

There are so many ways you can use potpourri, not only to scent your house during the holidays, but to add visual touches as well. And what could be more festive than an attractive container chock-full of greenery, pinecones, rich colored spices such as nutmeg, cinnamon, allspice, and brilliant red winter berries? Since potpourri takes about a month to mellow and season, the time to start your holiday potpourri is about four to six weeks before Christmas.

Once you've decided upon a particular holiday potpourri, or for that matter on several different concoctions, use your imagination and your collection of Christmas decorations to enhance the display. Why not place a few favorite Christmas tree ornaments in and around your potpourri? Gleaming gold, silver, blue, red, or green balls, or perhaps an antique family heirloom ornament or two, add festive touches to your holiday decor.

When you start to make your holiday potpourri, keep in mind that there is no set way to make any variety of potpourri. Within the range of each type of material, there are many options. For example, in a winter potpourri, you will want to use evergreen cones. Depending on what part of the country you live in, you might use cones from pine, hemlock, redwood, or balsam.

Many plants sport red berries during the winter, among them the hollies, barberry, firethorn, and wild rose. All are useful in potpourri. And there are many broadleaved evergreens that dry well. Don't limit yourself to following these recipes to the letter. If you don't have a particular ingredient, or can't lay your hands on it, you can substitute something that is available in your area, either growing in the wild or on your own property.

The same holds true for the oils that are called for in each recipe. You might decide, for example, that in the Holiday Spice potpourri, you prefer nutmeg or allspice oil to cinnamon oil, or a combination of allspice, nutmeg, and clove oils. The recipes that follow offer guidelines for you. In other words, don't be afraid to experiment with the plant material and oils available to you.

After the holidays, when you may want a change of scent in your house, simply pack up each potpourri separately in plastic bags and store them away. Next year check to see if the scent is still strong and, if not, add some oil to revitalize the potpourri.

Holiday Spice

· · ·

You probably have some of the ingredients for this potpourri right on your spice shelf, but if not, they are readily available at your local supermarket. One of the ingredients called for is red cedarwood chips. Around the holiday season, these are often available in gift shops or department stores. If not, and you decide that you wish to use them in a potpourri, they are easily made at home. Your local lumberyard offers cedarwood. Beg or buy a small piece and, using a carpenter's plane, take shavings of the wood off the piece. Break these into smaller pieces and dye them with red vegetable dye. When they assume a brilliant red color, remove them from the dye and let them dry.

As an option for red color, dried red celosia can be used, as can any of the many red berries from such plants as holly, barberry, wild rose, or firethorn. Bright red rose hips, which appear on wild or old-fashioned variety rosebushes after the roses lose their petals, in the fall in most parts of the country, will retain their color if you shellac them after picking.

3 tablespoons chopped orris root
½ teaspoon cinnamon (cassia) oil
20 cinnamon sticks
10 whole nutmegs
10 bay leaves
½ cup whole allspice
10 small pine, balsam, or other cones
2 to 3 cups red-dyed cedar chips or 1½ to 2½ cups dried broadleaved evergreen leaves such as holly, boxwood, or firethorn and ½ cup dried red holly, barberry, or wild rose berries, or ½ cup shellacked rose hips or ½ cup dried red celosia

1. Place the orris root in a quart-sized glass or porcelain jar with the cinnamon oil and mix thoroughly with a wooden spoon or chopstick. Cover the container with a lid and put aside for three days to allow the oil to absorb into the fixative. Shake every day.

2. After three days, pour the fixative-oil combination into a large glass or porcelain bowl. (Do not use a metal bowl, as the scent will be affected.) Then add all the remaining ingredients but the cedar chips and mix thoroughly.

3. Add enough cedarwood chips or substitute to make 1 quart of potpourri. Mix thoroughly.

4. Place the potpourri in the jar and cover. Let sit for one month in a dark place. Every few days either shake the jar or mix the potpourri with a wooden spoon or chopstick. After two weeks the potpourri should have a strong cinnamon scent.

If you like, at this point you can add nutmeg or allspice oil. Avoid using clove oil as its scent is overpowering. You may also want to experiment with adding powdered nutmeg, cinnamon, or allspice; however, keep in mind that your potpourri will have a dusty appearance if you use too much.

5. After one month, place the potpourri in a favorite container, decorate with some Christmas ornaments or greenery, and display.

I place this potpourri in an open antique mahogany box and add several small, feathered, handmade birds on top, which delights visitors during the holidays.

The bright red cedar chips of Holiday Spice Potpourri make it particularly festive, while its luscious scents of nutmeg, cinnamon, and allspice conjure up memories of holiday baking past.

Traditional Christmas Potpourri

. . .

We all know that the three wise men brought frankincense and myrrh as gifts to honor the infant Jesus. But how many of us know what they smell like? Here is an easy-to-make potpourri that can be enjoyed for its scent and beauty, and provides first-hand, for adults and children alike, the aroma of frankincense and myrrh.

3 tablespoons chopped orris root
½ teaspoon frankincense or myrrh oil
1 cup dried artemesia leaves
1 cup dried rosemary leaves
½ cup dried red berries (barberry, wild rose, holly)
1 tablespoon chopped frankincense or myrrh, the larger the pieces, the better visually
2 cups dried broadleaved, evergreen leaves such as English, Korean, Japanese, or Chinese boxwood, holly, or firethorn

1. Place the orris root in a quart-sized glass or porcelain jar with the frankincense or myrrh oil and mix thoroughly with a wooden spoon or chopstick. Cover the container with a lid and put aside for three days to allow the oil to absorb into the fixative. Shake every day.

Traditional Christmas Potpourri, made with frankincense and myrrh, is welcome in any holiday scene.

2. After three days, pour the fixative-oil combination into a large glass or porcelain bowl. (Do not use a metal bowl, as the scent will be affected.) Then add everything but the evergreen leaves and mix thoroughly.

3. Add enough of the evergreen leaves, about 2 cups, to make 1 quart of potpourri. Mix thoroughly.

4. Place the potpourri in the jar and cover. Let sit for one month in a dark place. Every few days either shake the jar or mix the potpourri with a wooden spoon or chopstick. After two weeks the potpourri should have a strong frankincense or myrrh scent. If not, add another ½ teaspoon oil to the mixture.

5. After one month, place the potpourri in a favorite container.

Since the wise men also brought Jesus a gift of gold, you might want to place some small gold balls in the potpourri. Or, if you have figurines of the Magi, you can place them in or near your potpourri arrangement.

Bayberry Potpourri

. . .

What could be a more classic holiday scent than that of bayberry? We've all enjoyed the scent of bayberry candles during the holiday season and now, with a bayberry potpourri, you can scent any room in the house with this lovely fragrance.

3 tablespoons chopped orris root
½ teaspoon bayberry oil
1 cup chopped cedarwood chips

½ cup berries, orange firethorn preferred—
however, red bayberry, holly berries, or
wild rose can also be used

½ cup bayberries (if you can't find
bayberries, you can use juniper berries,
usually available in health food stores, or
cedar berries)

2 cups dried bayberry or cedar leaves, if
available, or broadleaved evergreen leaves
such as English, Korean, Japanese, or
Chinese boxwood, holly, or firethorn

1. Place the orris root in a quart-sized glass or porcelain jar with the bayberry oil and mix thoroughly with a wooden spoon or chopstick. Cover the container with a lid and put aside for three days to allow the oil to absorb into the fixative. Shake every day.

2. After three days, pour the fixative-oil combination into a large glass or porcelain bowl. (Do not use a metal bowl, as the scent will be affected.) Then add everything but the bayberry leaves and mix thoroughly.

Bayberry candles are part of every Christmas celebration, so why not further enhance your holidays with Bayberry Potpourri?

3. Add enough of the dried bayberry or cedar leaves, about 2 cups, to make 1 quart of potpourri. Mix thoroughly.

4. Place the potpourri in the jar and cover. Let sit for one month in a dark place. Every few days either shake the jar or mix the potpourri with a wooden spoon or chopstick. After two weeks potpourri should have a strong bayberry scent. If not, add another ½ teaspoon oil to the mixture. You might also want to add ½ teaspoon of cedar oil.

5. After one month, place the potpourri in a favorite container and add your own personal Christmas decorating touches to it. You might also wish to place some bayberry candles near the potpourri.

Holiday Conifer Potpourri

. . .

The fresh scent of pine, balsam, or hemlock potpourri can be used all winter long in your house, not just during the holiday season.

3 tablespoons chopped orris root
½ teaspoon pine, balsam, or hemlock oil
1 cup dry pine or yew needles (these dry to a rich green. You can use blue spruce needles for a blue-toned potpourri. Unfortunately, balsam and hemlock dry brown)
½ cups dried red berries, such as barberry, holly berries, or wild rose berries
½ cup small pine or other evergreen cones
2 cups dried broadleafed evergreen leaves such as English, Korean, Japanese, or Chinese boxwood, holly, or firethorn

1. Place the orris root in a quart-sized glass or porcelain jar with the oil and mix thoroughly with a wooden spoon or chopstick. Cover the container with a lid and put aside for three days to allow the oil to absorb into the fixative. Shake every day.

2. After three days, pour the fixative-oil combination into a large glass or porcelain bowl. (Do not use a metal bowl, as the scent will be affected.) Then add everything but the evergreen leaves and mix thoroughly, using a wooden spoon or chopstick.

3. Add enough of the evergreen leaves, about 2½ cups, to make 1 quart of potpourri. Mix thoroughly.

4. Place the potpourri in the jar and cover. Let sit for one month in a dark place. Every few days either shake the jar or mix the potpourri with a wooden spoon or chopstick. After two weeks potpourri should have a strong pine, balsam, or hemlock scent. If not, add another ½ teaspoon oil to the mixture.

5. After one month, place the potpourri in a favorite container and decorate. Small silver and blue Christmas balls are particularly effective with this potpourri.

Sources for Planting Material

❦

Beyond your local nurseries and garden centers, there are hundreds of sources for planting material, but the following are pertinent to installing a potpourri garden. Write and ask them to send their catalogues; most are free.

Annual, Perennial, and Herb Seeds

George W. Park Seed Co., Cokesbury Rd., Greenwood, SC 29647-0001. In business since 1868, Park offers a large selection of annual, perennial, and herb seeds as well as plants, shrubs, bulbs, and a limited selection of roses, both standard and Miniature.

Thompson & Morgan, Box 1308, Jackson, NJ 08527, or call (800) 274-SEED, outside New Jersey, between 8:30 A.M. and 8:00 P.M. from January through March, and 8:30 A.M. to 5:00 P.M. from April through December. One of the largest selections of seeds available in the country.

W. Atlee Burpee Co., 300 Park Ave., Warminster, PA 18974. In business since 1876, this company offers a large selection of annual and herb seeds, some perennial and herb plants, as well as standard and Miniature roses and shrubs.

Bulbs

Van Bourgondien Bros., Box A, 245 Farmingdale Rd., Rte. 109, Babylon, NY 11702, or call (800) 645-5830 outside of New York, (800) 832-5689 in New York only. Probably the most comprehensive offering of Dutch bulbs, both spring-blooming and summer-blooming. Prices are among the most reasonable around.

Herb Plants

Nichols Garden Nursery, 1190 N. Pacific Hwy., Albany, OR 97321. A comprehensive selection of both herb seeds and plants, one of the largest purveyors of this material.

Perennials

Bluestone Perennials, 7211 Middle Ridge Rd., Madison, OH 44057. One of the best sources for perennial and herb plants at very reasonable prices. These are small plants, available in either three-packs or six-packs. All plants are guaranteed to reach you in good condition and to grow. If they do not, the company will reship immediately or refund your money if you are not satisfied.

White Flower Farm, Rte. 63, Litchfield, CT 06759-0050. A broad selection of perennial plants and shrubs. Expensive, but plants are well-established. Catalogue costs $5 but contains a great deal of valuable information.

Roses

Jackson & Perkins Co., Box 1028, Medford, OR 97501. The largest grower of rosebushes in the country. They offer Floribundas, Grandifloras, Hybrid Teas, Miniatures, Climbers, and shrub roses; however, they do not carry old-fashioned roses.

Roses of Yesterday and Today, 802 Brown's Valley Rd., Watsonville, CA 95076. This house offers a comprehensive selection of old-fashioned roses and some difficult-to-find modern roses.

Scented Geraniums

Shady Hill Gardens, 821 Walnut St., Batavia, IL 60510. Offers the largest selection of scented geranium plants in the country. Prices are very reasonable.

Shrubs

Girard Nurseries, P.O. Box 428, Geneva, OH 44041. A wide selection of azaleas and rhododendrons at very reasonable prices.

Kelly Nurseries, Dansville, NY 14437, or call (800) 828-6977, in New York (800) 462-6836. Interesting selection of shrubs.

Sources for Potpourri Material

⟡

Beyond local health food, herb, or craft shops, here are sources for materials you will need when you start creating your potpourris.

Caswell & Massey Co. Ltd., Catalogue Division, 111 Eighth Ave., New York, NY 10011. Without question, carries the finest available oils in the country. Prices are higher than elsewhere, but worth every penny in terms of purity and lasting fragrance. Among those offered are an intoxicating strawberry, mimosa, frangipani, fougere, heliotrope, bergamot, sandalwood, and honeysuckle. Also offers dried material such as cut myrrh, frankincense, tonka beans, orris root, and dried lavender, chamomile, and lemon verbena.

Claire Burke Home Fragrance, Minnetonka, MN 55343. They do not have a direct-mail business; however, their products are available in most fine department stores. It is worth the effort to seek out their peach oil.

Indiana Botanic Gardens, P.O. Box 5-HA, Hammond, IN 46325. An old-fashioned company offering an extensive list of oils and other potpourri materials. Prices are reasonable.

Penn Herb Co., Dept. HA, 603 N. 2nd St., Philadelphia, PA 19123. Another old-fashioned company offering oils and other potpourri materials. Prices are reasonable.

San Francisco Herb Co., 250 14th St., San Francisco, CA 94103. You can order a catalogue by calling their toll free number (800) 227-4530, in California (800) 622-0768. They offer many different oils and potpourri materials and include free potpourri recipes in their catalogue mailing. Prices are reasonable.

Scarborough & Co., Wilton, NH 03086. This company offers sachets, scented pillows, and scented drawer paper; however, their metal light bulb rings, which you place on a light bulb and moisten with a few drops of essential oil, are unique. Used in tandem with an open potpourri to enhance or intensify a scent, they offer yet another way of scenting a room.

Tom Thumb Workshops, P.O. Box 332, Chincoteague, VA 23336. This company offers an extensive list of essential oils and dried material such as yucca pods, lotus pods, and many dried flowers. Prices are reasonable.

Index